GREAT BRITISH JOURNEYS

RICHARD MADDEN

GREAT BRITISH JOURNEYS

A Bucket List of Unforgettable Trips

Published by National Trust Books
An imprint of HarperCollins Publishers,
1 London Bridge Street London SE1 9GF www.harpercollins.co.uk

HarperCollins Publishers,
Macken House, 39/40 Mayor Street Upper, Dublin 1, D01 C9W8, Ireland

First published 2026
© National Trust Books 2026
Text © Richard Madden 2026
Illustrations © Sara Mulvanny 2026

ISBN 978-0-00-877287-1

10 9 8 7 6 5 4 3 2 1

All rights reserved. No part of this publication may be reproduced, stored in a retrieval system, or transmitted, in any form or by any means, electronic, mechanical, photocopying, recording or otherwise without the prior permission in writing of the publisher and copyright owners.

Without limiting the exclusive rights of any author, contributor or the publisher of this publication, any unauthorised use of this publication to train generative artificial intelligence (AI) technologies is expressly prohibited. HarperCollins also exercise their rights under Article 4(3) of the Digital Single Market Directive 2019/790 and expressly reserve this publication from the text and data mining exception.

The contents of this publication are believed correct at the time of printing. Nevertheless, the publisher can accept no responsibility for errors or omissions, changes in the detail given or for any expense or loss thereby caused.

A catalogue record for this book is available from the British Library.
Printed by Multivista Global Pvt. Ltd, India.

If you would like to comment on any aspect of this book, please contact us at the above address or national.trust@harpercollins.co.uk

National Trust publications are available at National Trust shops or online at nationaltrustbooks.co.uk

Contents

Introduction 6

Wonderful Walks 9

Unforgettable Train Journeys 67

Remarkable Road Trips 119

Beautiful Boat Rides 181

Index 234

Introduction

'The geography of Britain is like a poem written in earth, stone, and water.' I'm not sure whether this observation by my school geography teacher struck me as remarkable at the time. Or even if it is a well-known quotation whose source I have still not identified. Either way, it has remained firmly lodged in my memory.

Over the many years that have passed since I first heard those words, I have been lucky enough to experience for myself just how true they are. Whether it be driving along the ancient drover roads that snake across the Scottish Highlands; gazing out over the Irish Sea from the carriage windows of a train skirting the coast of Wales; opening a lock gate on the Shropshire Union Canal; or putting one foot in front of the other along a pilgrim path followed by countless generations of travellers, each mode of transport offers its own unique lens through which to discover more of the country.

The forty Great British Journeys collected in this volume are divided into the four primary modes of travel: Wonderful Walks, Unforgettable Train Journeys, Remarkable Road Trips and Beautiful Boat Rides. All, however, are more than mere instructions on travelling from point A to point B. They are invitations to slow down, to notice, to connect with both landscape and heritage in ways that our increasingly hurried world rarely permits. Every mile of every route has witnessed human drama played out across centuries. Kings and commoners, soldiers and sailors, pilgrims and merchants have all contributed to the rich tapestry of British experience that these excursions reveal.

Walking, the original form of human travel, offers the most direct connection to the surrounding landscape. From following the coast around Cornwall's Lizard Peninsula to taking on the eight peaks of the Fairfield Horseshoe in the Lake District, the routes gathered here include gentle rambles that can be enjoyed by families as well as challenging mountain traverses that test both stamina and navigational skills.

Rail travel is a uniquely civilised experience, allowing passengers to watch the countryside unfold like a moving painting. The railway journeys in this book celebrate Britain's pioneering role in the age of steam and steel. They include both the West Highland Line, carrying *The Jacobite* steam train (a.k.a. the 'Harry Potter Train' or 'Hogwarts Express'), and the East Coast Main Line between Newcastle and Edinburgh, with its inspirational views over the North Sea coastline and inland over Northumbria and the Scottish borders.

Road trips hold a special appeal that invite spontaneity. They become an adventure in themselves and not just a means of reaching a destination. Whether exploring the geological marvels of the Jurassic Coast in Dorset or taking on the North Coast 500 – 'Scotland's answer to America's Route 66', as it is often known – the freedom of the open road allows travellers to immerse themselves in unfamiliar landscapes.

The waterways of Britain offer a unique passage through time. Canal boat journeys showcase the industrial archaeology of Britain's eighteenth-century transport system. Following serene canals that whisper tales of the Industrial Revolution, and rivers that have shaped cities and powered the growth of a nation, the aquatic routes in this book provide a unique perspective on the country's heart and soul, their ancient locks and aqueducts standing as monuments to a bygone era.

Walking routes. Rail journeys. Road trips. Waterways. Only one question remains: which will you explore first?

Wonderful Walks

From the majestic landscapes of the Scottish Highlands to the rolling hills of the South Downs, Britain is home to some of the world's most diverse walking experiences. All the more remarkable given that they are to be found in such a relatively small area.

Whether you're steeling yourself for the rocky summit of Yr Wyddfa (Snowdon), contemplating a tranquil meander around the honey-stone villages of the Cotswolds or exploring the wild beauty of Northumberland's borderlands, our islands offer a mosaic of unique environments to explore on foot.

Most of the walks featured here can be completed in a single day. So lace up your boots, pack your waterproofs (this is Britain, after all), and prepare to discover why generations of walkers have found adventure and inspiration in the footpaths, bridleways and mountain tracks that crisscross our glorious countryside.

View from Quiraing
Old Man of Storr (p.62)

Summit
Devil's Staircase (p.58)

Lindisfarne Castle
St Cuthbert's Way (p.46)

Gordale Scar
Malham Cove (p.34)

View from High Pike
Fairfield Horseshoe (p.40)

Herefordshire Beacon
Malvern Hills (p.30)

Crib Goch
Yr Wyddfa (Snowdon) Horseshoe (p.52)

Kynance Cove
Lizard Point (p.12)

Snowshill Manor
Broadway Tower (p.24)

Cuckmere Haven
Seven Sisters (p.18)

Lizard Point, Cornwall

Britain's most southerly circuit

Although many are lured by the siren song of Land's End to the west, the Lizard Peninsula – the most southerly point in the UK – is, along with its surrounding bays, coves, inlets and moorlands, one of the most bewitching stretches of coastline in Britain. This 7-mile (11-km) circular walk starts from Kynance Cove and follows the South West Coast Path (SWCP) to Lizard Point before heading east past its lighthouse to Bass Point, then north-west through Lizard village itself and back to the start.

Below: The path down to the beach at Kynance Cove, Cornwall.
Opposite: The rugged coastline at Kynance Cove.

Kynance Cove is an artwork as much as a beach. It was voted among the Top 50 Best Beaches in the World (2024), and its name is derived from the Cornish Porth Keynans, meaning 'ravine cove'. Best viewed from the cliffs at Tor Balk to the west, the beach is laid out between its trio of rocky outcrops: Asparagus Island, Gull Rock and the pointed mitre of the Bishop. Kynance Cove has been a favourite spot for day trippers since Victorian times, and many of its surrounding caves have names from that era, such as the Ladies' Bathing Pool, the Parlour and the Drawing Room.

The coastline here is also famous for its serpentine – a metamorphic rock identified by its green shades veined with white, cream or red streaks, reminiscent of snakeskin from which its name is derived. In spring and summer, the wild flowers explode in splashes of blues, yellows, whites and pinks worthy of a Jackson Pollock painting, and with equally spectacular

Below: View from Lizard Point.
Opposite: Flowering heather on the cliffs near Kynance Cove.

Wonderful Walks

names. Squill, dropwort, bloody crane's-bill, lady's bedstraw and selfheal all thrive here. Heading south, look out for seals and basking sharks, the latter sometimes up to 30ft (9m) long. The Lizard is also a birder's paradise, with buzzard, peregrine falcon, raven and stonechat all regulars alongside gannet, shearwater and guillemot further offshore.

After passing Lizard Point itself, a now disused Victorian lifeboat station can be seen from above Polpeor Cove on the southernmost cliff face. The treacherous Cornish coastline has seen many shipwrecks over the centuries and the Lizard Peninsula is no exception. Its lighthouse, built in 1752, has twin towers originally lit by coal-fired braziers and once described by the poet Alfred, Lord Tennyson as 'the southern eyes of England'. These days the lighthouse is automated, with only one tower lit. It also has an electronic fog signal 30 times louder than a pneumatic drill. The light itself is so powerful that it can be seen from 26 nautical miles out at sea.

Continue on to Lion's Den, a 39ft (12m) hole in the cliff created when a cave collapsed one night in the mid-1800s, and on to the headland at Pen Olver. Here, two black huts mark one of the sites that pioneering radio engineer Guglielmo Marconi used for his early experiments. Marconi believed that radio signals could be transmitted around the curvature of the Earth and, in January 1901, he received a message here that had travelled 186 miles (300km) from the Isle of Wight – a new distance record. Marconi also built a much larger radio station 6 miles (10km) away at Poldhu from where the first transatlantic transmissions were made. The National Trust restored Pen Olver station in 2000 and the two buildings have now been converted into a holiday let and a museum. From Lloyd's Signal Station at Bass Point, head left inland to Lizard village and over the village green before taking the path back towards Kynance Cove.

Opposite top: Footpath at Bass Point looking towards Lizard Lighthouse.
Opposite bottom: The Lloyd's Signal Station at Bass Point where semaphore communications were once made with vessels entering the English Channel.

Seven Sisters, East Sussex

White cliffs roller-coaster

Haven Brow, Short Brow, Rough Brow, Brass Point, Flagstaff Point, Flat Hill, Bailey's Hill, Went Hill Brow. The names of the hills that cap the gleaming chalk cliffs standing sentinel over the English Channel between Seaford and Eastbourne don't quite have the romantic ring of the Seven Sisters who, in Greek mythology, immortalised the star cluster we now know as the Pleiades. And confusingly, there are actually eight cliffs – not seven.

Starting from around 100 million years ago, they were created during the

Below: View from Cuckmere Haven towards the white cliffs of Birling Gap.
Opposite: Walking the Seven Sisters looking towards Belle Tout Lighthouse in the distance.

Cretaceous period by the skeletons of minute coccoliths and single-celled planktonic green algae sinking to the seabed, forming lime mud and hardening into chalk before being thrust upwards by movements in the Earth's crust. Their average rate of growth is estimated to have been around half an inch (1.25cm) every thousand years. A quick calculation reveals that Beachy Head above Eastbourne – at 531ft (162m) the highest chalk sea cliff in Britain – took around 13 million years to grow. The undulating valleys and the series of bays that separate the cliffs were formed by a combination of glacial meltwater at the end of the last Ice Age and gradual erosion by the sea. Nature's works of art don't just happen overnight.

Hardly surprising then that the iconic vista looking east from Cuckmere Haven, with the Coastguard Cottages in the foreground, was for a while one of the most popular landscape screen savers on computers around the world. It has also been used as a backdrop in films, from the Harry Potter movies to *Hope Gap* and *Atonement*.

The terrain on this 13-mile (21-km) walk, starting from Seaford and ending in Eastbourne, varies between the short urban stretches along the seafronts of both towns; the climb up from Seaford and down into Eastbourne; the undulating white paths along the grassy covering of the cliffs themselves; and the shingle on the beach at

Right: Birling Gap, looking back along the Seven Sisters towards Cuckmere Haven.

Cuckmere Haven. The latter requires either wet feet, negotiating the River Cuckmere itself as it rushes into the sea, or a short detour inland at high tide.

Landmarks along the way include the Martello tower in Seaford, the most westerly of a series of 103 fortified structures built in England in the first years of the 19th century to protect against invasion during the Napoleonic era; Birling Gap with its National Trust café and shop; and Belle Tout Lighthouse, built in 1832 and decommissioned in 1902 before being moved back 56ft (17m) from the eroding cliff edge in 1999 to stop it toppling into the sea. Possible bird sightings along the way include swallows, peregrine falcons, kittiwakes and fulmars depending on the time of year, with Adonis blue and common blue butterflies often seen in summer.

Left: Approaching Eastbourne at the end of the Seven Sisters walk.
Above: Beachy Head and the Belle Tout Lighthouse.

Wonderful Walks

Broadway Tower, Cotswolds

A Cotswolds classic

The village of Broadway itself sets the tone for this classic 4-mile (6.5-km) circular walk. Often referred to as the 'Jewel in the Crown' of the Cotswolds, Broadway offers everything that makes the surrounding National Landscape (formerly Area of Outstanding Natural Beauty) so unique, from honey-coloured limestone houses dating back to the 16th century, to boutique hotels, tea-rooms and the rolling hills that surround it. The walk described is just one of many possible circular routes of varying lengths around Broadway.

Above: The atmospheric village of Broadway, Worcestershire.
Opposite: At 65ft (20m) the Broadway Tower, with its three Saxon-style turrets, crowns the second-highest hill in the Cotswolds.

At 65ft (20m), Broadway Tower crowns the adjacent peak. The second-highest hill in the Cotswolds, it was once the site of a beacon warning of the approach of the Spanish Armada in 1588. A unique example of the architectural genius of the Georgian era, the tower was conceived by the legendary landscape designer Lancelot 'Capability' Brown and commissioned in 1798 by the 6th Earl of Coventry for his wife Barbara, Lady Coventry. It was then built by the architect James Wyatt. The tower is constructed in hexagonal Saxon-era style, with three round turrets at the corners complete with battlements and gargoyles.

One theory for its purpose – assuming it had one – is as a beacon that Lady Coventry could see from her house 15 miles (24km) to the north-west. On a more practical level, it was later used as a country retreat by Pre-Raphaelite artists, including William Morris. Today, the tower has a museum on three floors and a roof-top platform with views that stretch more than 60 miles (97km) across 16 counties, reaching as far as the Black Mountains of South Wales and the Long Mynd in Shropshire. Beneath the tower, there is a relic from the Cold War – a nuclear bunker!

The walk starts in Broadway at the village green lined with chestnut trees; the path heads south along the High Street before meeting the Cotswold Way and winding through open fields towards Broadway Hill and the climb to the tower. The nearby woodlands are home to oak, ash and beech trees and the meadows are speckled with

Right: Snowshill Manor, cared for by the National Trust, houses Charles Paget Wade's collection of historic crafts and artefacts.

wildflowers in spring and summer including the yellows and pinks of cowslip, primrose, field scabious and bird's-foot trefoil, as well as rare species such as the pasqueflower with its purple bell-like flowers. The rare Adonis blue butterfly can also sometimes be seen.

After your visit to the tower, head south to the village of Snowshill. Just north of the village its manor house, now in the care of the National Trust, houses Charles Paget Wade's eclectic collection of crafts, artefacts and curiosities. Outside are gardens designed to reflect the construction of the house itself in a series of outdoor rooms. In the village, St Barnabas Church is a Victorian masterpiece built in medieval style. Snowshill is also famous for its lavender fields at Hill Barn Farm to the east of the village – usually at their peak between mid-June and early August.

After following the path west again to the top of Shenberrow Hill, the final leg heads north back to Broadway where the journey began, passing ancient stone walls and more stunning views of the Cotswold escarpment.

Above: The gardens of Snowshill Manor.
Opposite top: Lavender fields at Hill Barn Farm in full summer bloom.
Opposite bottom: The village of Snowshill with St Barnabas Church at its centre.

Wonderful Walks

Malvern Hills, Herefordshire and Worcestershire

Inspiration to creative genius

This spectacular 9-mile (14.5km) walk through the Malvern Hills – a National Landscape (formerly Area of Outstanding Natural Beauty) on the border between Herefordshire and Worcestershire – passes through some of England's most captivating landscapes, a mix of open grasslands, rolling hills, woodland and rugged peaks. Many famous composers and writers have been inspired by the Malvern Hills, including Sir Edward Elgar (*Enigma Variations* and *The Dream of Gerontius*); J.R.R. Tolkien (*The Lord of the Rings*); and the 14th century poet William Langland (*The Vision of Piers Plowman*).

While the total distance is moderate, the cumulative elevation gain of

approximately 1,970ft (600m) makes this a challenging walk requiring good fitness levels. From Great Malvern, a good place to start this north-to-south walk is St Ann's Well, which houses the source of the famous Malvern Water. From here many paths wind their way up directly to Worcestershire Beacon or back to North Malvern for those who want to complete the full end-to-end trail.

From the latter, a number of paths climb through woodland before crossing a grassy bank between the summits of Table Hill and North Hill and following a level track beside the Sugarloaf. The trail emerges onto the exposed ridge at Worcestershire Beacon, the highest point in the Malvern Hills at 1,394ft (425m). From the summit on a clear day, the cathedrals of Worcester, Gloucester and Hereford are all visible, with the view extending across the Severn Valley to the Cotswolds in the east and the Brecon Beacons in the west.

The undulating main ridge now continues past Summer Hill and then descends towards the Wyche Cutting before climbing again towards Perseverance Hill and Jubilee Hill through sections of woodland interspersed

Above: The view at dawn over the Malvern Hills looking north from British Camp (Herefordshire Beacon), an Iron Age hill fort.

with open grassland. After crossing the A449, the path reaches British Camp, also known as Herefordshire Beacon, one of the most impressive Iron Age hill forts in the country and for many the highlight of the walk. Dating from the 2nd century BC and covering 32 acres (13ha), the earthwork ramparts remain clearly visible, creating a series of defensive rings around the hilltop. Archaeological evidence suggests continuous occupation from the Iron Age through to the Roman period. Some believe this is where the chieftain Caratacus made his last stand against the Romans.

After British Camp, the trail then continues southwards over a number of peaks and saddles before ending at Chase End Hill at the southern end of the Malvern Hills. Along this section the local geology becomes apparent; exposed rock faces reveal the igneous and metamorphic rocks, thrust up along an ancient fault line at least 650 million years ago, that form the backbone of the hills. These ancient formations, among the oldest in England, create the distinctive steep-sided profile that makes the ridge line visible from such a long way off.

Depending on onward travel arrangements, one option is to descend on the western edge, anywhere along the route after Jubilee Hill. A network of paths lead to Colwall station, which provides an alternative starting or ending point for those using public transport. Following clear paths through woodland and pasture, this descent takes approximately 30–45 minutes.

Left: The view at sunrise looking north from Worcestershire Beacon, the highest point on the Malvern Hills at 1,394ft (425m).

Malham Cove, Yorkshire Dales

Nature's artwork

If anywhere can be said to characterise the Yorkshire Dales, it is the village of Malham and the geological artworks to be found in the surrounding countryside. Across the nearby fields, criss-crossed with the area's signature stone walls, you'll encounter: Janet's Foss, a woodland waterfall, home to a legendary fairy queen; Gordale Scar, a flooded limestone ravine; and the star of the show, Malham Cove itself.

Below: Historic packhorse bridge crossing Malham Beck.
Opposite: Janet's Foss: a waterfall over a limestone outcrop and home to a fairy queen.

Formed at the end of the last Ice Age more than 12,000 years ago, when glacial meltwater thundered through the valley, Malham Cove is named after its curving vertical face, 262ft (80m) high and 984ft (300m) wide, and visible from miles around. Nearby is tranquil Malham Tarn, the highest natural lake in England, home to endangered water voles and other rare aquatic species.

The 8-mile (13-km), 4–5 hour circular walk from Malham takes in some of the most inspiring landscapes and geological features in the Yorkshire Dales. After crossing Malham Beck, the Pennine Way leads to Janet's Foss where water plunges over a limestone outcrop into the pool below. Surrounded by fern and moss-covered trees, with the refreshing scent of wild garlic in the spring, it is a wonderfully inviting spot.

Above: The view from the waterfall at Gordale Scar.
Opposite: The limestone cliffs of Malham Cove from below.

Further up the valley is Gordale Scar, a deep, rock-scattered ravine created by glacial meltwater during successive Ice Ages. It is thought to have been J.R.R. Tolkien's inspiration for Helm's Deep in *The Lord of the Rings* and was also the subject of a painting by J.M.W. Turner in 1816. After leaving the ravine the path now heads up the steep hillside towards the top of Malham Cove.

Having reached the summit of this limestone amphitheatre, crossing it feels like walking to the centre of a giant stage. A rendition of *Hamlet*'s 'To be, or not to be' soliloquy may feel appropriate. From a geological perspective, the Cove is classified as a limestone pavement, which consists of blocks known as 'clints' and fissures known as 'grikes', the latter created by rainwater seeping through the cracks. The result looks not unlike fossilised dinosaur footprints. Whatever the appropriate simile, the artistry of geological time is evident.

From the Cove, it's just a short walk over the moors to nearby Malham Tarn, one of the highest lakes in Britain. A Site of Special Scientific Interest (SSSI) and a Special Area of Conservation (SAC), the tarn covers an area of around 150 acres (60ha) and is home to many submerged aquatic plants, including stonewort algae which provides habitat and food for other organisms and contributes to water quality. It is also home to six fish species, and bird life that includes the great crested grebe, moorhen, coot, tufted duck and teal. Last, but certainly not least, is the water vole, which was reintroduced in 2016. If you spot a few of the above on the way up, the way down back to Malham on the other side of the valley will feel like a victory lap.

Below: Malham Tarn: a Site of Special Scientific Interest (SSSI) and a Special Area of Conservation (SAC).

Fairfield Horseshoe, Lake District

Ambleside spectacular

Beginning and ending in Ambleside at the northern end of Lake Windermere, the Fairfield Horseshoe is an 11-mile (18-km) circuit that perfectly illustrates why the Lake District has captured the imagination of visitors for centuries.

Traversing a series of eight summits in a sweeping arc around the head of the Rydal valley – including several featured in Alfred Wainwright's *A Pictorial Guide to the Lakeland Fells*, published during the 1950s and 60s – this is a journey through some of England's most sublime mountain scenery.

With an elevation gain of more than 3,000ft (900m), the eight peaks it takes in are: Nab Scar, Heron Pike, Great Rigg, Fairfield, Hart Crag, Dove Crag, High Pike and Low Pike. The route has a few rocky sections and can be boggy underfoot in wet weather but on a clear day is very easy to follow. Walkers should allow 6–7 hours and be equipped for a challenging walk.

Opposite: Dove Crag, at 2,598ft (792m), is one of eight Wainwright summits on the Fairfield Horseshoe.
Above: The view from Nab Scar above Rydal Water with the summits of Loughrigg and Wetherlam beyond.

Taking the clockwise route, the adventure begins with a gentle ascent north from Ambleside towards Low Sweden Bridge over the River Rothay. The path rises steadily through ancient oak woodland after which the first real climb begins on the southern slopes of Nab Scar, with the dramatic profile of Heron Pike beckoning the traveller onwards and upwards along the ridge. As you climb higher, the sweeping views over Rydal Water and Grasmere start to reveal themselves.

The horseshoe proper begins while crossing the ridge from Heron Pike to Great Rigg, the path now a high-level promenade above the valleys. Ascending towards the summit of Fairfield, the shimmering waters of Windermere and the patchwork of valleys open out below. Approaching the crest, the vastness of the Lake District unfolds in a sprawling tapestry of rolling fells and glistening lakes. The summit of Fairfield (2,864ft/873m) is a magnificent vantage point, the monarch of this particular mountain kingdom. The peak has one of the finest views in the Lakes and is one of the best places to absorb the atmosphere of the high fells.

Above: The view over Heron Pike with Lake Windermere in the background.
Opposite: Looking north towards Great Rigg and Fairfield (under cloud). A section of the walk with some of the best views in the Lake District.

The descent from Fairfield towards Hart Crag marks the horseshoe's northern arc, where the landscape takes on a wilder, more remote character. The path picks its way across rocky terrain, past hidden tarns, with the summit of Hart Crag providing another spectacular vantage point. Here, the dramatic south-eastern face of Helvellyn dominates the horizon. As you continue along the ridge towards Dove Crag, the horseshoe begins its eastern sweep. This is one of the most thrilling ridge walks in the Lakes, made up of narrow paths between rocky outcrops with steep drops into the adjacent valleys.

The final summits of High Pike and Low Pike complete the horseshoe's eastern arm, each offering its own unique perspective on the surrounding scenery. The long descent back towards Ambleside carries you through a changing landscape, from the stark beauty of the high fells, through the rolling pastures of the middle slopes and finally into the sheltered woodlands of the valley floor.

Below: Lake Windermere from High Pike looking over Low Pike on the eastern arm of the Fairfield Horseshoe.

Wonderful Walks

Above: The ruins of 12th-century Melrose Abbey. It was here that St Cuthbert began his religious odyssey c. AD 650.

St Cuthbert's Way, Northumbria

Pilgrim trail

Before pilgrimages were banned by Henry VIII in 1538, there were many well-trodden routes up and down the land leading to sacred destinations. These were walked both as an act of faith and also as a way of finding relief from the struggles of day-to-day life. For many of us, over five centuries later, their purpose has never felt more relevant.

This 62-mile (100-km) route on the Scottish Borders begins at the Gothic ruins of 12th-century Melrose Abbey, where St Cuthbert began his religious odyssey *c.* AD 650. The path, which was inaugurated in 1996, crosses the Eildon Hills, where there is an ancient hillfort, the Tweed Valley and the foothills of the Cheviots before reaching Lindisfarne, the saint's initial burial place, just off the Northumberland coast. Most people walk west to east, which follows the chronology of St Cuthbert's life, but the route is waymarked in both directions.

After Melrose, the trail ascends through woodland and open fields, crossing the col between the three Eildon Hills. It then follows stretches of the River Tweed and Dere Street, an

ancient Roman road. Along the way is 15th-century Cessford Castle with its massive L-shaped fortifications, after which the path crosses a beautiful hill ridge leading to the village of Kirk Yetholm. The route then climbs the northern edges of the Cheviot Hills, passing the village of Hethpool before descending into the fine old market town of Wooler.

From Wooler, the landscape gradually opens out onto expansive moorlands and farmland before descending the winding track through conifer trees to St Cuthbert's Cave, a rock-lined cavern hidden under the overhang of an escarpment. It was here that the monks of Lindisfarne are said to have rested overnight with the uncorrupted body of St Cuthbert on the way to Durham Cathedral for reinterment in a shrine. Religious graffiti, some of it centuries old, has been carved into the sandstone rocks.

A distinctive feature of this section of the trail is the intense colour in spring and summer of wild

Above: Signpost on St Cuthbert's Way above the village of Kirk Yetholm in the Scottish borders.
Right: View from the village of Hethpool in the College Valley on the edge of the Cheviot Hills.

flowers, including bluebells, primroses, wood anemones and wild garlic. Birdsong is also a constant companion to the travelling pilgrim: everything from chiffchaffs and meadow pipits to skylarks, curlews and lapwings. As the path reaches the coast, seals, puffins, guillemots and terns take centre stage. The dramatic finale across the causeway to the Holy Island of Lindisfarne – where St Cuthbert was abbot – is only possible at low tide. The sand flats are punctuated by wooden marker poles known as pilgrim posts.

The ruins of the historic Benedictine priory, founded by St Aidan in the 7th century, soon come into view, a testament to the island's early Christian heritage. The Parish Church of St Mary the Virgin has a life-size wooden sculpture of St Cuthbert's funeral cortege. Towering above them both is Lindisfarne Castle, the 16th-century fortress converted by Sir Edwin Lutyens into a private home, and now in the care of the National Trust, with its beautiful Edwardian interiors, and its extensive gardens designed by Gertrude Jekyll.

Below: The ruins of the Benedictine priory with Lindisfarne Castle beyond.
Opposite: Lindisfarne Castle, the 16th-century castle now cared for by the National Trust, with the ruins of the Benedictine priory in the foreground.

Yr Wyddfa (Snowdon) Horseshoe, Gwynedd

The great Welsh challenge

Seven miles (11km) may not sound like a long way for a day walk. But add in an ascent of just over 3,280ft (1,000m), along with some sheer ridges and rocky scrambles, and even the hardiest hiker might be tempted to think again. This horseshoe route to the top of Yr Wyddfa (Mount Snowdon), the highest peak in Wales (3,560ft/1,085m), also includes three other summits: Crib Goch

Above: The Pen y Pass car park with the Crib Goch ridge towering above.
Opposite: The Crib Goch ridge is classed as a Grade I Scramble.

(3,028ft/923m), Garnedd Ugain (3,494ft/1,065m) and Y Lliwedd (2,946ft/898m). As always, there's the ever-changing weather to think about. To stay safe, you'll need essentials such as sturdy hiking boots, layered clothing, a first-aid kit, map, compass, water and high-energy snacks. Physical endurance and mental focus are non-negotiable. A spectacular adventure it may be, but the demanding nature of this hike is not to be underestimated.

    There are a number of routes to the summit of Yr Wyddfa. This one begins from the Pen y Pass car park, taking the Pyg Track followed by an ascent of Crib Goch. Known for its knife-edge ridge and breathtaking views, this is the most challenging section of the horseshoe. Hikers are confronted with a rock-strewn path that grows ever steeper the higher it climbs, fluctuating between a simple hike and a more technical scramble. The famed Crib Goch ridge is classed as a Grade 1 Scramble, which means using your

hands to stay balanced in some sections as well as sure-footedness and a head for heights due to the sheer drops on either side. Weather conditions can significantly affect the level of difficulty. On a clear day, however, it rewards with some truly epic views.

At the end of Crib Goch the descent into the Bwlch Coch saddle offers a brief respite. From here, the climb up Garnedd Ugain (the summit of Crib-y-Ddysgl ridge) is less intimidating with a rocky but broad path that opens out to reveal some landscape masterpieces in the valleys below. The final ascent towards the summit of Yr Wyddfa involves a series of switchbacks with some scrambling sections thrown in for good measure.

As you approach the summit the views expand dramatically, with the lush

Above: The view from the summit of Yr Wyddfa overlooking Lyn Llydaw.

valleys, distant lakes and rolling hills creating a backdrop that will linger long in the memory. On a clear day you can see as far as Ireland, Scotland and the Isle of Man. The summit can be busy on a summer's day, courtesy of the legendary Snowdon Mountain Railway, but now is the time for that celebratory photo alongside Yr Wyddfa's distinctive circular stone trig point.

After leaving the summit, the path leads south-east to the rocky ridge of Y Lliwedd. This section has beautiful views over the waters of Glaslyn and Llyn Llydaw with its surrounding peaks and valleys. As you begin your descent the trail winds along the ridge of Bwlch Main, notorious for its narrowness and steep drops on either side. The trail eventually begins to widen, however, leading to the intersection at Bwlch Ciliau. Steep grassy slopes descend to Cwm Dyli but for this walk head north-east towards the Miners' Track and around Llyn Teyrn lake, then back to the car park at Pen y Pass.

Above: Hiker on the Pyg Track passing Lyn Llydaw near Pen y Pass.
Right: The peaks of Y Lliwedd from the Miners' Track over the waters of Llyn Teryne.

The Devil's Staircase, West Highland Way

Pathway to heaven

The Devil's Staircase is one of the most beautiful sections of the West Highland Way, the long-distance 96-mile (154-km) footpath between northern Glasgow and Fort William in the Scottish Highlands. It was given its name by soldiers carrying heavy materials to construct a military road in the 18th century. Its original purpose was to allow quicker access into the Highlands for English troops following the Jacobite Rebellions of 1715 and 1745.

When walking south to north, the trail starts on the A82 to the east of Glencoe at the foot of Buachaille Etive Mòr. It then snakes its way upwards to a high point of 1,800ft (550m) before descending to the village of Kinlochleven. While certainly challenging, this 5-mile (8-km), 4-hour hike is one of the best day walks in the area thanks to the Highland views it offers.

The path is well-trodden but uneven, with rocky outcrops and loose stones requiring careful footing. The gradient starts gently but becomes steeper before gradually turning into a series of sharp zigzags, which were the only way military supply vehicles were able to make it to the summit.

At the top of the Devil's Staircase on the Aonach Eagach ridge, the highest point along the West Highland Way, the views are glorious: Buachaille Etive Mòr to the south; Rannoch Moor to the east; the Mamores ridge to the north; and Glencoe to the west. The summit is marked by a small cairn. On a clear day you can also see the unmistakeable profile of Ben Nevis behind the Mamores, with patches of snow lingering in the corries even during summer. The water shimmering in the gaps between the peaks ahead and to the right

Left: Altnafeadh at the foot of Buachaille Etive Mòr, the start of the Devil's Staircase.

is the Blackwater Reservoir, with the longest dam in the Highlands at over 3,000ft (900m) long.

As you descend, spectacular views open up across the Mamores mountain range to the north and Loch Leven stretching eastward through the glen. The path gradually transitions from exposed moorland to more sheltered terrain as you lose altitude. Ancient Scots pines begin to appear along the route and small burns cascade down the hillside. The final approach to Kinlochleven follows the old drove road through gentler slopes covered in heather and bracken.

The village of Kinlochleven sits at the head of Loch Leven, historically significant for its aluminium smelting industry. The path begins a long, slow descent to Kinlochleven; it passes close to the Blackwater Reservoir, built

between 1905 and 1909 for a hydroelectric plant in the valley. The route runs briefly along a rock ledge on the side of the hill to a footbridge over a burn. The pipes from the reservoir come into view and the route winds through woodland of predominantly silver birch trees. Head directly downhill close to the pipeline before crossing the River Leven just past the former aluminium smelting plant, now the Ice Factor National Ice Climbing Centre and a microbrewery.

Opposite: Cairn at the summit of the Devil's Staircase, looking west towards Glencoe.
Below: Kinlochleven with Loch Leven beyond, seen from the top of the Devil's Staircase.

Wonderful Walks

Old Man of Storr and the Quiraing, Isle of Skye

When the Skye's the limit

The Isle of Skye off Scotland's rugged north-west coast is the largest island in the Inner Hebrides. Its landscapes have been shaped over aeons by a combination of volcanic activity, glacial erosion and landslides. These events have turned massive rock formations into some of nature's most dramatic artworks. Chief among them are the Old Man of Storr and the Quiraing.

Located on the Trotternish Peninsula in the far north, the former is a 160-ft (49-m) basalt rock pinnacle, rising out of softer sedimentary rocks, that is thought to be a volcanic plug. These are created when magma hardens within the vent of an active volcano. The Quiraing, which is still experiencing movement to this day, is a grassy crater on the eastern slopes of Meall na Suiramach (1,782ft/543m). It surrounds a labyrinth of leaning lava rocks and weathered buttresses resulting from the largest landslip ever seen in the British Isles.

Left: Sunrise over the Quiraing – part of the Trotternish Ridge, which was formed by the largest landslip ever seen in the British Isles.

The name Quiraing is derived from the Old Norse term 'Kví Rand', meaning 'Round Fold', said to relate to an era when the local farmers hid their cattle here to shield them from Viking invaders. Several of the Quiraing's formations have acquired nicknames relating to their appearance over the centuries. The Prison resembles a medieval fortress with its pyramid-shaped rocky peak; the Needle is a 120-foot- (37-m) high spire jutting out above a sloping bed of scree; the Table is a flat area of grass that has separated from the summit in aeons past. The Quiraing's cliffs and crevices attract golden eagles to its rocky crags; lower down, the chirrups of the tiny meadow pipit can often be heard.

One popular 5¼-mile (8½-km) walking loop around the Quiraing starts at the (often crowded!) car park on the Quiraing Road off the A855 in the far north of the peninsula. The journey begins with a moderately easy walk beneath cliffs, passing the Prison and the Needle, before ascending steeply to the ridge and Meall na Suiramach's peak. Throughout the trail, there are views of the Quiraing and the surrounding landscapes, and on clear days the mainland can just be seen beyond the Sound of Raasay. The path can be treacherous in wet weather and requires a head for heights. A steep and sometimes slippery descent leads back to the starting point.

The Old Man of Storr is reached from a marked parking area on the A855. The path, which combines stairs and rocky sections, ascends for about 30 minutes before the pinnacle comes into view; sturdy hiking equipment is required due to the uneven terrain. Hikers should ignore paths to the left, which take a detour around a neighbouring hill. Instead, keep straight ahead until the path curves left around the southern side of the rock. Finally, make a right turn and continue the ascent along the western side. A narrow passage between the cliff and a boulder offers a remarkable view. Further on still the track forks right around the northern side of the pinnacle leading back on a circular route to the start. However, keep straight ahead for the best panoramic view of them all at the Storr Lookout Point, with Loch Leathan and the waters of Bearreraig Bay providing the perfect backdrop.

Opposite: The Old Man of Storr is thought to be a volcanic plug rising out of softer sedimentary rocks that have eroded away.

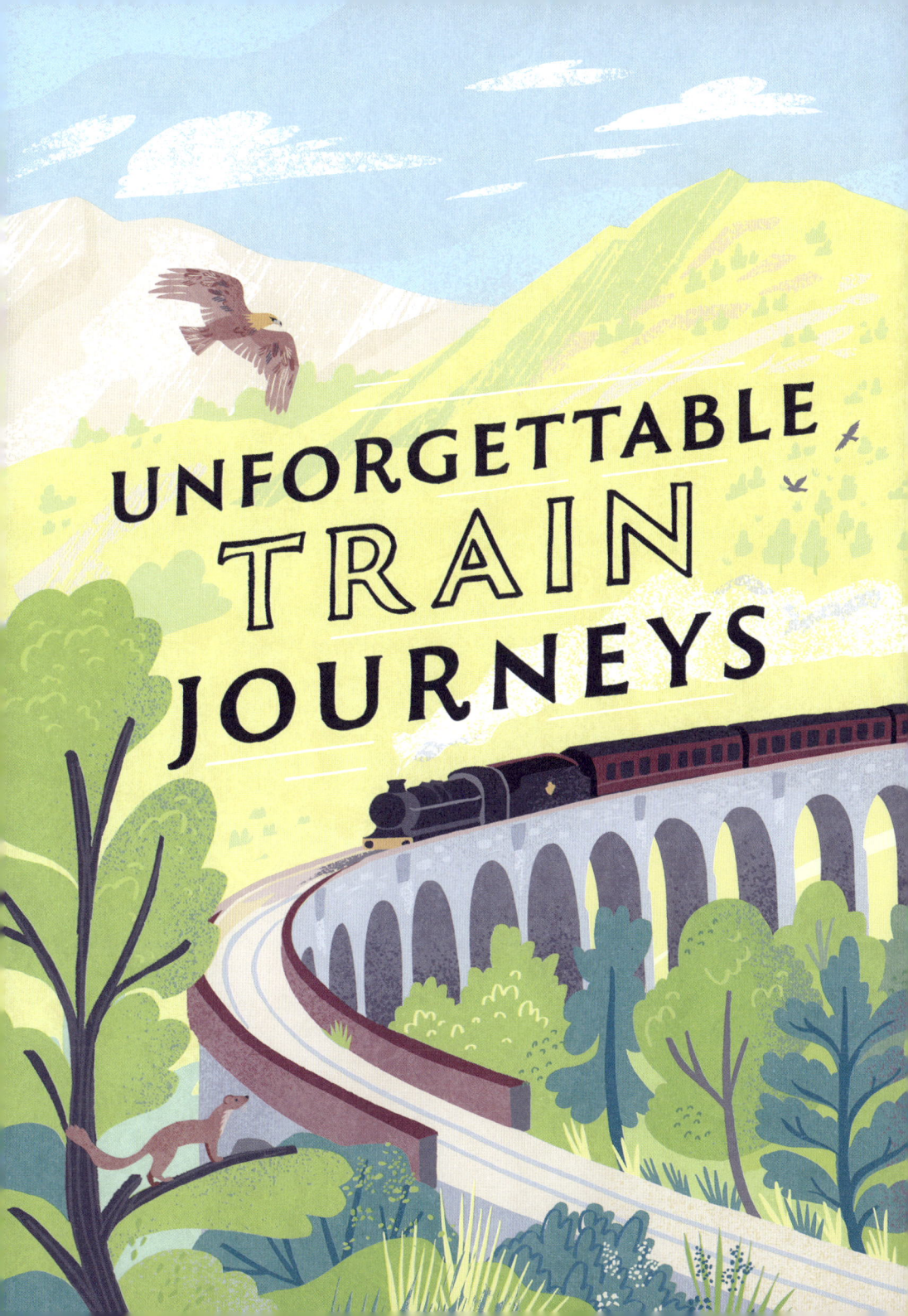

Unforgettable Train Journeys

Britain was the birthplace of the railways, and the train lines that traverse these islands have witnessed more than two centuries of history. The best are voyages through time itself, past medieval castles perched on clifftops and into cities where Roman walls stand sentinel beside the glass towers of the modern age.

Each line has its own character, and its own particular genius for revealing the hidden Britain that lies between the well-trodden tourist paths. You can find it in the wild romance of the Settle-Carlisle line through the Yorkshire Dales or the willow-lined riverbanks beside Devon's Tarka Line.

The whistle has blown, the guard has waved their flag, and one of the greatest shows on earth – the British landscape in all its moods and seasons – is about to begin.

Glenfinnan Viaduct
West Highland Line (p.108)

Attadale
Kyle of Lochalsh Line (p.114)

Morecambe Bay
Bentham Line (p.82)

Alnmouth
East Coast Main Line (p.92)

Ascending Yr Wyddfa
Snowdon Mountain Railway (p.104)

Ribblehead Viaduct
Settle to Carlisle Railway (p.86)

Barmouth
Cambrian Coast Line (p.98)

Barnstaple
Tarka Rail Line (p.70)

Worcester
Cotswold Line (p.78)

Horsted Keynes
Bluebell Railway (p.74)

Tarka Rail Line, Devon

Tales of the riverbank

The Tarka Line, officially known as the North Devon Line, runs 39 miles (63km) from the city of Exeter in South Devon to Barnstaple in the north of the county, following the river valleys of the Yeo and Taw. Opened in 1854, it adopted the name 'Tarka Line' in 2001 to recognise the author Henry Williamson, whose classic tale *Tarka the Otter* is set in rural Devon. With a journey time of 75 minutes, the line joins the beginning and end of the sinuous 180-mile (290-km), figure of eight, Tarka Walking Trail.

Above: Platform 5 at Exeter St David's station.
Right: Tarka Line train heading towards Barnstaple.

The villages and towns along the line are well worth exploring in themselves, all steeped in history with many medieval churches and market squares. After leaving Exeter St David's station with views of the River Exe, the line is soon surrounded by rolling hills and lush fields. The train first stops at the village of Newton St Cyres, whose church dates back to the 14th century. At Crediton, on the banks of the River Creedy where it joins the River Yeo, the history of the church can be traced back to the early 10th century. The town is also famous for being the birthplace of St Boniface, one of the most significant figures in early European Christianity.

Beyond Crediton, the Tarka Line runs towards the River Taw with distant views of Dartmoor to the south-west. As the valley widens, the train crosses numerous small bridges over tributaries and streams among the area's network of waterways. One of the most enjoyable parts of the journey is crossing the River Taw, which the line follows for a significant portion of the route. Multiple bridges cross the river and its willow-lined tributaries.

Approaching Copplestone, the landscape grows wilder with oak trees and thatched cottages lining the track. One of Copplestone's most notable features is its ancient cross, a ninth-century granite pillar believed to have been a

boundary marker or memorial stone. Lapford's Church of St Thomas of Canterbury is another of the area's medieval churches, this one dating back to the 12th century. The area around Eggesford is home to the country's first state-owned forest planted by the newly created Forestry Commission in 1919; this enchanting woodland is visible from the train.

Nearing Barnstaple, the landscape broadens: the River Taw once more flows alongside the line before it widens into estuaries, home to herons and kingfishers among the riverbank willows. Barnstaple itself is famous for its Pannier Market, a name that dates back to Victorian times when panniers were used to carry goods to market on the backs of pack animals. With its proximity to Exmoor National Park and the North Devon coast, the town is an ideal base for exploring the great outdoors, including stunning beaches and rugged coastline. The perfect end to a journey that typifies the serene beauty of rural Devon.

Opposite: Tarka Line train crossing the River Taw.
Below: The River Taw and Holy Trinity Church, Barnstaple.

Bluebell Railway, East Sussex

Time travel by steam engine

Did someone mention *Doctor Who*'s Tardis? Surely not. In the 21st century, vintage steam trains are by far the most reliable form of time travel. Nothing stirs the imagination more than the sight and sound of hissing plumes of steam, high-pitched whistles, a shining brass bell and the chug and clank of an engine slowly but surely gaining speed. And look, over there! It's the Railway Children in Victorian garb waving wildly from the side of the track.

The start of the Bluebell Railway, the UK's first preserved standard-gauge passenger railway, is located just around the corner from the National Trust gardens at Sheffield Park in East Sussex. The 22-mile (36-km) round-trip train ride to East Grinstead takes approximately 45 minutes each way and is the perfect option for a leisurely day-trip. Restored to its 1880s grandeur, Sheffield Park station is a portal into a bygone era complete with vintage signs and advertisements, leather-clad

Right: Bluebell Railway steam train approaching Sheffield Park station.

red seats in the waiting room and station staff in period uniforms. But then again, perhaps you've simply stumbled into the opening scene of a Sherlock Holmes mystery.

But now we're off! As the guard raises a green flag and blows the whistle, sliding compartment doors, polished wood panelling, springy seats and gleaming brass welcome you into the golden age of rail travel. And should you need it, there's plenty of room for top hats and bonnets. Soon the green and pleasant fields of England start flowing by. In spring, blossom adorns the

Opposite: Bluebell Railway steam train approaching Kingscote station.

Right: Tudor timber-framed building in the town of East Grinstead at the end of the Bluebell Line.

hedgerows and bluebells carpet the floor of the adjacent woodland, while shafts of sunlight pierce the overhanging trees.

Seen from a steam train, the world beyond looks entirely different from the view we're used to on modern commuter trains, with their crowded open-plan seats. And for an extra touch of indulgence, there's a cream tea service available on select departures. Freshly baked scones, clotted cream and strawberry jam taste even better when paired with the gentle swaying of the carriages and a steaming cup of tea from The Grinsteade Buffet.

Horsted Keynes, the next station on the line, has five platforms restored in 1930s style together with a carriage and wagon workshop, making it the largest preserved heritage railway station in the UK. The Bluebell Line has featured in many films and a sudden gasp of recognition awaits *Downton Abbey* fans when they find themselves pulling into 'Downton Station'. A much-prized example of period railway architecture, Horsted Keynes is also a magnet for steam railway enthusiasts.

Travelling northwards once more, one of the line's most memorable views awaits as the South Downs rise up over the Weald below. Kingscote, the next station, fast forwards into the aura of the 1950s; in winter the coal fire in the booking hall is lit to offer a warm welcome to travellers. Reaching the terminus at East Grinstead, the journey culminates in a market town steeped in the even deeper past and a High Street that is home to one of the longest stretches of 14th-century timber-framed buildings in England.

Cotswold Line, Oxford to Worcester

Quintessential English countryside

'Yes. I remember Adlestrop.' The first line of Edward Thomas's poem about his journey on a steam train through the Cotswolds on 24 June 1914 memorably evokes a lost idyll of the English countryside shortly before the outbreak of the First World War. Although the poem itself was not written until after war had broken out, Thomas wrote down in his notebook his impressions of the grass, the willows, the willowherb and meadowsweet, the

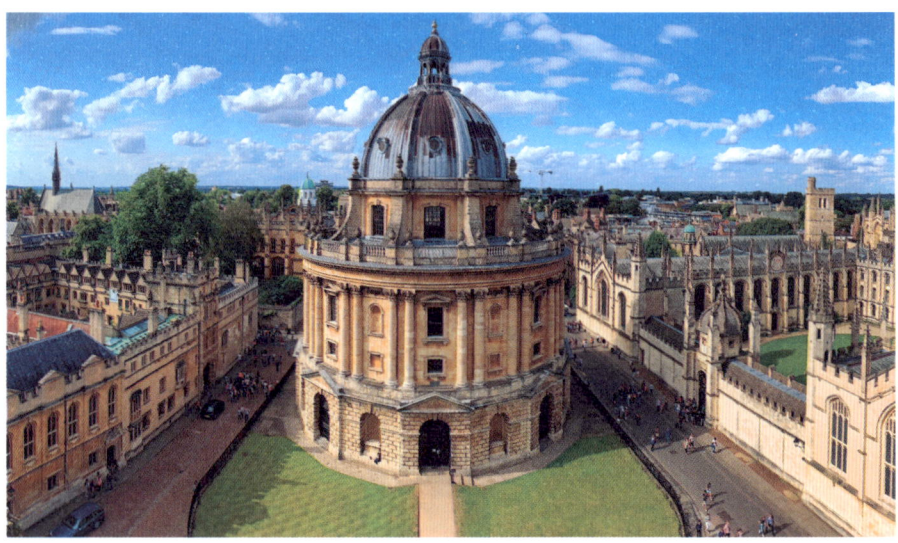

Above: The Bodleian Library's Radcliffe Camera in Radcliffe Square, Oxford.
Opposite: View over wheat fields near Charlbury in the Cotswolds.

blackbirds and the silence interrupted by the hiss of steam, which he later included in the poem.

Today the station is long gone, although the ADLESTROP sign that once stood on the platform can still be seen at a bus stop in the village. The poem conjures up a powerful sense of the English countryside, which can still be enjoyed from the windows of the train that runs through the Cotswolds from Oxford to Worcester, a journey of just over 50 miles (80km) that takes around an hour and 15 minutes. On the hundredth anniversary of the original journey, an 'Adlestrop Centenary Special' train transported 200 passengers from Oxford to Moreton-in-Marsh, stopping at the former site of Adlestrop station.

A train journey through the Cotswolds, a National Landscape (formerly Area of Outstanding Natural Beauty), is at its best and most colourful in spring. Hedgerows are dense with hawthorn and cherry blossom, and fields of bright yellow rapeseed illuminate the landscape. Occasionally, a solitary oak stands sentry, its ancient limbs stretched wide and strong, while bluebells carpet the surrounding woodlands.

Leaving the 'dreaming spires' of Oxford itself, the track meanders north as allotments and industrial estates slowly give way to green fields, rolling hills, thatched cottages and glimpses of ancient church spires above the treeline. Stone walls built from the region's distinctive honey-coloured limestone begin

to appear. The approach to Hanborough brings the first true taste of Cotswold character. This is followed three stops later by Charlbury with its Georgian and Victorian cottages alongside medieval buildings, their rooflines creating the town's distinctive, irregular skyline. Beyond Kingham station, the Cotswold landscape is at its glorious best. Drystone walls climb impossible gradients as yet more church spires rise above the canopies of trees surrounding hidden villages.

The approach to Moreton-in-Marsh brings the most dramatic scenery of the journey. The train curves through a cutting where wild flowers have colonised the embankments as ash and beech trees envelop the train. At Honeybourne, the surrounding countryside begins its subtle transformation from classic Cotswold views into the fruit-and-vegetable-producing landscapes of Worcestershire.

The fields grow larger as stone walls give way to post-and-rail fencing, and the honey-coloured limestone is gradually replaced by red-brick farmhouses. Eventually, Worcester's suburbs come into view, overlooked by the Malvern Hills. The city's distinctive skyline is dominated by the spire of Worcester Cathedral – the final resting place of King John of Magna Carta fame.

Opposite: Thatched cottages in the Cotswold village of Kingham.
Below: Worcester Cathedral by the River Severn.

Bentham Line, North Yorkshire Moors and Lancashire

The 'Little North Western'

Unforgettable Train Journeys

Opposite: Steam train near Hellifield in Yorkshire where the Bentham Line begins its western descent.

Left: Skipton Station is often referred to as the 'Gateway to the Dales'.

The 75-mile (120-km) Bentham Line, often referred to as the 'Little North Western' after the railway company that constructed it, crosses the Pennine Hills in the heart of Yorkshire and parts of Lancashire. Opened in June 1850, it was one of the first railways in Britain, designed to connect rural communities to the city of Leeds. It is also one of England's most scenic routes. The 2-hour journey showcases the diversity of northern landscapes, from the urban energy of Leeds through the limestone of the Yorkshire Dales, the farming country of the Lune Valley, historic Lancaster and on to the coastal drama of Morecambe Bay.

It departs from Leeds, after which the city's suburbs gradually give way to the approach to the Yorkshire Dales. The first stretch passes through Shipley, where the River Aire meanders alongside the tracks, and past Keighley. Now the terrain begins its transformation from post-industrial Yorkshire into the landscape beyond Skipton, often referred to as the 'Gateway to the Dales'.

At this point the train begins its climb through Gargrave, where limestone walls criss-cross the countryside. This is the Craven district of Yorkshire where the geology shifts dramatically and the landscape opens out into broad valleys. The line then curves through Hellifield where it begins its western descent, following ancient packhorse routes through Giggleswick with its trademark stone cottages and the silhouette of Ingleborough (2,372ft/723m), the second-highest mountain in the Yorkshire Dales, on the skyline. Here, the line skirts the northern end of the Forest of Bowland, a National Landscape (formerly Area of Outstanding Natural Beauty), with woods and moorlands stretching as far as the eye can see.

The landscape begins to soften approaching Clapham, where limestone ridges give way to the gentler contours of eastern Lancashire. Bentham marks the crossing of the county border into Lancashire, a transition both geographical and cultural. The train passes through High Bentham, a small market town that serves the surrounding farming community, before continuing its westward journey through increasingly lush countryside. The approach to Lancaster follows the River Lune, one of England's most beautiful, yet least celebrated, rivers. The valley here is broad and fertile, with the Pennines gradually receding and the Lake District fells beginning to appear on the northern horizon.

Lancaster's cathedral and castle soon dominate the skyline as the River Lune curves around the city's edge, with glimpses of the Lancaster Canal – a

remarkable feat of Georgian engineering that once connected the city to the wider world of industrial Britain.

The final stretch to Morecambe crosses an area of coastal plain, past Heysham Power Station and through the suburbs that mark the transition from countryside to seaside resort. The air begins to carry the salt tang of Morecambe Bay with its beautiful views but treacherous sands, which are infamous for their shifting channels and dangerous tides. On clear days, the Lake District fells rise dramatically across the water, with the distinctive profile of the Old Man of Coniston clearly visible.

Above: Morecambe Bay beach and marshland.

Settle to Carlisle Railway, Yorkshire Dales and North Pennines

Railway masterpiece

This historic line runs 72 miles (116km) through some of the most mesmerising landscapes in the Yorkshire Dales and North Pennines, from the market town of Settle in North Yorkshire to the city of Carlisle in Cumbria. Taking on average an hour and 50 minutes, its landmark stone viaducts and tunnels are an enduring testament to the genius of Victorian engineering.

Overcoming considerable challenges, its original purpose was as a commercial lifeline transporting coal and limestone from remote rural communities to the city. Narrowly surviving the infamous Beeching cuts of the 1960s, two decades later it faced closure once more due to declining use, outdated infrastructure and the financial pressures of maintaining such an isolated route. Ultimately it was saved, in recognition of the historical and cultural importance of Britain's railway heritage.

North of Settle, with its cobbled streets and 'Derby Gothic' station, the train makes its way into open countryside, the Pennines providing a dramatic backdrop and setting the tone for the journey ahead. The landscape here – a patchwork of fields peppered with rocky outcrops and punctuated by isolated farmhouses – is criss-crossed by drystone walls and cloaked in heather.

Left: The 24 arches of the Ribblehead Viaduct cross more than 400 yards (366m) of moorland in the Ribble Valley.

Above: Settle station in North Yorkshire at the southern end of the line.

Above: Steam train crossing the Garsdale viaduct, also known as the Dandry Mire Viaduct.
Opposite: A Tornado steam locomotive bursts out from the Blea Moor Tunnel.

The line is famous for its architectural masterpieces, most notably the Ribblehead Viaduct with its 24 arches crossing more than 400 yards (366m) of moorland in the Ribble Valley. Along with the Glenfinnan Viaduct in Scotland, it is one of the most photographed stretches of railway line in the British Isles. As the train approaches, the sheer scale of the construction becomes evident with views of the Yorkshire Three Peaks – Whernside, Ingleborough and Pen-y-ghent – dominating the horizon.

Beyond the viaduct each twist and turn reveals something new, from the meandering rivers to the escarpments that rise abruptly from the valley floor, and heather-clad moorlands, valleys and ancient woodlands. After passing through Horton-in-Ribblesdale and Ribblehead itself, we arrive at the village of Dent, known for its cobbled streets and historic buildings.

Further north, the train reaches the Blea Moor Tunnel – one of 14 tunnels on the entire route, all remarkable feats of engineering burrowing beneath the moorland. Its exit opens out onto sweeping views of Dentdale and the River Dee. Finally, the train begins its descent into the Eden Valley dotted with villages and historic towns, including Appleby-in-Westmorland with its ancient castle.

As the train pulls into Carlisle station near the Scottish border, passengers are greeted by the sight of the city's famous castle, a brisk 15-minute walk away. After surviving seven sieges by the Scots between 1174 and 1461, it later held Mary, Queen of Scots as a prisoner. Alongside Carlisle's many surviving medieval buildings are ruins from its previous incarnation as the Roman city of Luguvalium. A fitting conclusion to an historic rail journey.

Left: Train driver aboard a Stanier Class 8F steam locomotive.
Below: *Union of South Africa* steam locomotive at Carlisle station.

East Coast Main Line, Newcastle to Edinburgh

Bordering on the sublime

Above: The Tyne Bridge (background) and Gateshead Millennium Bridge (foreground) crossing the River Tyne between Newcastle and Gateshead.
Opposite: St Cuthbert's Cross overlooking the estuary at Alnmouth.

The East Coast Main Line from London to Edinburgh, which opened in the mid-19th century, is one of the UK's busiest railway lines. A section of this line, the 90-minute, 124-mile (200-km) journey between Newcastle and Edinburgh Waverley stations, is also one of the most scenic on the entire British rail network. Its views look out over the North Sea coastline and inland over the landscapes of Northumbria and the Scottish borders.

Departing from Newcastle, the line heads north through the industrial landscapes of Tyneside, with the famous Tyne Bridge visible to the south. The train passes through Morpeth as rolling hills gradually give way to moorland. As it approaches the coastline, the view opens out over sandy dunes to the seaside village of Alnmouth and Dunstanburgh Castle beyond. From Alnmouth, the tracks hug the coastline for much of the journey with views over rugged cliffs, sand dunes, windswept beaches and theatrical displays of surf crashing against rocks. As the train curves inland once more, Lindisfarne Castle, the 16th-century fortress now in the care of the National Trust, is visible in the distance.

The Scottish Borders region is dotted with sheep farms and stone cottages as the train reaches the historic fortress town of Berwick-upon-Tweed,

Unforgettable Train Journeys

complete with Elizabethan walls and the magnificent Royal Border Bridge, a viaduct with 28 arches opened by Queen Victoria in 1850. Its name often leads to confusion as the actual border between England and Scotland is approximately three miles further north. Depending on the weather, glimpses can be had of the region's four ruined abbeys (Melrose, Dryburgh, Kelso and Jedburgh), as well as Smailholm Tower, a fortified 'peel' tower near Kelso.

The line now begins to climb gradually as it approaches the volcanic, heather-clad slopes of the Lammermuir Hills in the west. As the train crests the hills and begins its descent towards Edinburgh, the character of the landscape changes. The wild Border country gives way to the more cultivated farmlands of East Lothian and Midlothian dotted with small towns and villages such as North Berwick, known for its conical volcanic hill, Berwick Law. Surrounded by nature reserves, the towns of Gullane and Aberlady Bay are edged by wide, sandy beaches and a first glimpse of coastal Scotland.

To the west, passengers are now rewarded with a first view of Edinburgh's skyline, dominated by the volcanic plug of Arthur's Seat and the silhouette of Edinburgh Castle itself. The train slows as it crosses the Forth Rail Bridge, providing a brief but magnificent view of the Firth of Forth.

Left: Dunstanburgh Castle was built in the 14th century to defend a headland on the Northumbrian coast.

Approaching Edinburgh Waverley, located between the medieval Old Town and the New Town, the train makes its way through Edinburgh's southern suburbs, passing Musselburgh and Portobello before curving around to approach the station from the east. Finally, it descends into the deep cutting that houses Edinburgh Waverley. As the train comes to rest beneath the glass roof of the station, passengers disembark into the very heart of Scotland's capital city.

Above: The Royal Border Bridge crosses the River Tweed 3 miles south of the England/Scotland border.
Opposite: Edinburgh skyline at sunset.

Cambrian Coast Line, Aberystwyth to Pwllheli

Wales's coastal extravaganza

The 36-mile (57-km) section of the Cambrian Coast Line from Aberystwyth to Pwllheli along the west coast of Wales is widely considered to be one of the most beautiful railway journeys in Britain. A showcase for the coastal scenery of Cardigan Bay, the 3-hour trip runs alongside wide beaches with distant panoramas of the mountains of Eryri (Snowdonia); it also crosses the famous Barmouth Viaduct across the Mawddach Estuary, offering frequent wildlife sightings of everything from bottlenose dolphins and seals to guillemots, razorbills and fulmars.

After leaving Aberystwyth and skirting the coastline at the village of Borth, the line runs inland along the estuary of the River Dyfi before meeting the main inland Cambrian Line at Dovey Junction and heading west again to the coast. This area is a haven for wildlife and home to diverse birdlife, including ospreys and herons.

As the train approaches Aberdovey, the line hugs the contours of the coastline with views of the Irish Sea on one side and the backdrop of Eryri

Left: View through a window at Aberystwyth railway station.

Right: The Cambrian Coast Line near Borth.

National Park on the other. Particularly striking is the stretch near Tywyn, with its connection to the Talyllyn steam railway. The line then passes through several small stations, including Tonfanau and Llwyngwril. Both stops provide access to coastal walks and beaches. The train often pauses at these stations for several minutes, allowing passengers time to appreciate the quiet coastal atmosphere.

The stretch between Fairbourne and Barmouth runs directly along the beach, separated from the sea by only a narrow strip of sand and shingle. Beachgoers, surfers and coastal wildlife are all visible from the carriage windows. Barmouth itself includes some of the line's most striking views as the train crosses Barmouth Bridge, a viaduct spanning the Mawddach Estuary. Opened in 1867, at 2,690ft (820m) in length, it is the longest timber viaduct in Wales and one of the oldest in regular use in Britain.

Above: The Cambrian Coast Line connects with the heritage Talyllyn narrow-gauge steam railway line.

Opposite: The railway bridge at Barmouth, crossing the Mawddach Estuary, is the longest timber viaduct in Wales.

As the train travels north it stops at Harlech, home to medieval Harlech Castle, built by Edward I during his conquest of Wales in the late 13th century and now a UNESCO World Heritage Site. The Llŷn Peninsula can now be seen unfolding ahead, with distant views of Yr Wyddfa (Mount Snowdon). Here the train stops at Porthmadog, the gateway to Eryri National Park. Continuing north it passes through Criccieth with views of Tremadog Bay and the surrounding hills. The town is dominated by the ruins of another 13th-century castle perched on a rocky outcrop overlooking the sea.

The landscape finally transitions into the Llŷn Peninsula itself, with its dramatic cliffs, secluded coves and sandy beaches. The peninsula is dotted with ancient sites, from Iron Age hill forts to early Christian monuments. Finally the train reaches Pwllheli where its marina is filled with yachts and fishing boats. Known for its lively markets and rich maritime history, the town is a fitting end to a memorable journey.

Right: Harlech Castle was built by Edward I in the late 13th century.

Snowdon Mountain Railway, Gwynedd

Train ride to the heavens

It all begins at Llanberis station, base camp for the spectacular 60-minute, 4.7 mile (7.6-km) train journey to the summit of Yr Wyddfa (Mount Snowdon). At 3,560ft (1,085m), Yr Wyddfa is the highest peak in Wales and England. And this is no ordinary train. The Snowdon Mountain Railway is an engineering marvel, the poster boy of the pioneering rack and pinion technology of the Victorian era.

Opened in April 1896, the railway was constructed to make Yr Wyddfa accessible to the general public. It runs from mid-May to the end of October, with the original steam locomotives operational between June and September working alongside more recent diesel engines. Each pushes a single carriage up the mountain and leads it down again, ensuring a controlled descent. Pre-booking is strongly advised.

As the train departs, the views from the vintage carriages slowly open out from an initial tunnel of trees onto secluded valleys dotted with grazing sheep. The hissing steam and rhythmic chugging quickly bring smiles to the faces of passengers as they embark on a shared adventure. Changing altitudes reveal different habitats, the lower moorland slopes dotted with ancient oak woodlands giving way to craggy rock faces as the train ascends. Soon the air becomes crisper and cooler as the Irish Sea makes a guest appearance in the west.

Opposite top: The Snowdon Mountain Railway on the way to the summit.
Opposite bottom: Approaching the summit station.

At Halfway Station, where the steam engines stop to refill their water tanks, passengers can spot walkers on Llanberis Path to the east. Here, as at other points along the way, the line splits briefly into two so that ascending and descending trains can pass. Beddgelert, one of the prettiest villages in Eryri (Snowdonia), is also visible on a clear day. A little further on, at Rocky Valley with its near-vertical drop, more stunning views appear. Higher still, Clogwyn station – the highest point trains can reach in spring when ice and snow are still on the ground – delivers panoramic views of Llanberis Pass and the jagged Crib Goch ridge. In this exposed part of the mountain the landscape is treeless and harsher – a stark contrast to the lush valleys below.

As the train climbs higher and higher, each twist and turn unveils a new masterpiece through the carriage windows, the views ever-changing as the horizon stretches further into the distance. Light and shade move through the landscape as clouds drift across the sky above, with the waters of Llyn Llydaw and Llyn Teyrn shifting in colour between dark blue, turquoise and silver.

From Summit station it is sometimes possible to see as far as the Isle of Man and Ireland. The summit building, Hafod Eryri (meaning 'high mountain dwelling in Snowdonia'), with its eco-friendly architecture, has touch-screen information panels and displays offering insights into the mountain's history, geology and culture. An interactive smartphone app is also available. All that remains now is the short walk to the summit itself in the crisp mountain air, followed by a steaming cup of hot tea or coffee at the café, and the opportunity to sit back and enjoy the matchless views over the mountain scenery below.

Opposite top: The Snowdon Mountain Railway with the Llanberis valley and spoil heaps of Dinorwig slate quarry in the distance.
Opposite bottom: The eco-friendly summit building, Hafod Eryri.

West Highland Line, Glasgow to Mallaig

All aboard the 'Hogwarts Express'

The West Highland Line, between Glasgow and the fishing port of Mallaig on the west coast of Scotland, has been hailed as the most scenic train journey in the world. Sections of the 5½-hour, 26-stop, 99-mile (159-km) line have featured in many films and documentaries, most famously the Harry Potter series in which Harry and Ron fly over Glenfinnan Viaduct on the way to Hogwarts in Arthur Weasley's flying car. *The Jacobite*, a steam locomotive now often called the 'Hogwarts Express', was introduced in 1984 to run alongside the more common diesel engines and quickly became a firm favourite.

    From Glasgow Queen Street station, the line heads north towards the Kilpatrick Hills with panoramic views of Erskine Bridge and a fleeting glimpse of thirteenth-century Dumbarton Castle, one of Scotland's oldest strongholds. The sea lochs of the Firth of Clyde are followed by Loch Long, named after the Viking longships that once invaded these waters. To the west are the Arrochar

Left: The Caledonian sleeper train crosses Rannoch Viaduct.

Unforgettable Train Journeys

Alps including The Cobbler, one of the most popular hill-walking peaks in Scotland. Next on the roll call of star names is Loch Lomond, once home to Scotland's favourite outlaw, Rob Roy McGregor. In the distance looms the peak of Ben Lomond itself.

At Crianlarich, where two glens collide, the line divides. The northern route continues to Fort William and Mallaig while the southern route travels on to Oban on the west coast. Heading north, the surrounding geography transitions from dense woodland to open moorland with a landscape dominated by mountains, lochs and views of the ruins of Kilchurn Castle, the 15th-century stronghold of Clan Campbell.

The train then glides around the head of Loch Awe before negotiating the Pass of Brander. This section is a gateway to the bleak beauty of Rannoch Moor – a patchwork of bogs, lochs and rocky outcrops covering more than 50 square miles (130 square km). The line continues to

Left: *The Jacobite* steam train near Corpach on the West Highland Line.
Above: The Corrour Summit is the highest and most remote point on the West Highland Railway.

Corrour, which, at 1,340ft (408m), is the highest and most isolated mainline station in the UK, accessible only by rail or on foot. At Tulloch, the line then curves westwards towards Fort William, gently descending to the shores of Loch Treig and through the narrow Monessie Gorge. Nearing Fort William, passengers can glimpse Ben Nevis, at 4,413ft (1,345m) the UK's highest peak.

The final, and most anticipated, section of the line between Fort William and Mallaig crosses the Glenfinnan Viaduct, an outstanding feat of Victorian engineering and the longest concrete railway bridge in Scotland. Built in the 1890s over the River Finnan 100ft (30m) below by Sir Robert 'Concrete Bob' McAlpine, the viaduct's 21 arches were constructed using the most advanced technology of the day.

The final stretch to Mallaig hugs the coastline, passing through Arisaig with views of the Small Isles of Rum, Eigg, Muck and Canna, and the white sands of Morar. As the sun sets in the west on a summer's evening, this transition from mountains to the rugged Atlantic shore is often a scene of heart-stopping beauty.

Opposite and top: *The Jacobite* steam train crossing the Glenfinnan Viaduct.
Above: The fishing port of Mallaig at the northern end of the West Highland Line.

Kyle of Lochalsh Line

Scottish Highlands coast-to-coast

This most rugged and beautiful of railway lines starts in Inverness, the 'Capital of the Highlands' on the east coast of Scotland, and travels 82 miles (132km) to the village of Kyle of Lochalsh on the west coast. The latter is just a mile across the water from Kyleakin on the Isle of Skye. On this 2½-hour journey passengers can enjoy views of some of the most scenic landscapes in Scotland, from forests and lochs to mountain peaks and remote villages, ending with views of the famous road bridge itself reaching over the sea to Skye.

Like other now celebrated scenic lines, it was originally built to boost trade and commerce – in this case between Inverness and remote rural locations. Completed in 1897, it still serves as an essential lifeline for many communities while also being a magnet for visitors wanting to experience the magic of the Highlands.

As the train heads west from Inverness, the urban outskirts of the city are gradually replaced by a unique cross-section of the landscapes of the Scottish Highlands. These start with views to the west over the Beauly Firth and to the east towards Kessock Bridge and the Moray Firth, an arm of the North Sea, followed by wide-open fields, dense forests and tranquil lochs. Mountains, their peaks often shrouded in mist, come into view as the train snakes its way through a series of deep valleys.

Opposite top: Train crossing the Plantation Viaduct near Achanalt on the Kyle of Lochalsh Line.
Opposite bottom: Train rounding the coast near Stromeferry.

Continuing along this remote terrain past atmospheric villages, passengers are treated to the sight of deep lochs reflecting both the sky and the dense forests carpeting the lower slopes of the mountains. The first notable stop along the route is Dingwall, a cultural centre and ancient Viking settlement, followed by the cavernous Strathpeffer Valley with its views of Ben Wyvis. Continuing west, the train reaches Garve, a small Highland village bordered by hills on the shores of the eponymous loch, followed by the journey's most dramatic section climbing through remote mountain terrain to Achnasheen and south-east to Strathcarron. At the latter comes a first glimpse of steely blue seawater lochs, their long fingers stretching inland from the ocean beyond.

Approaching the Kyle of Lochalsh itself, the line runs along the very edge of the rugged Scottish coastline as if teetering on the sea's edge. Meanwhile, Skye's unmistakeable Cuillin Mountains slowly become visible to the north-west. To the south, the Skye Bridge, often described as like a dragon's back, reaches out over the serenely beautiful Loch Alsh. Open to the elements and filled with the scent of salt and seaweed, the tiny port station itself carries a sense of history, having served for so many decades as a crucial link for inhabitants, tourists and goods travelling to and from the islands. It's the perfect finale to a journey on this historic railway line.

Left: *The Great Marquess* steam train near Attadale on the Kyle of Lochalsh Line.

REMARKABLE ROAD TRIPS

Remarkable Road Trips

In a country where the traveller is never more than 70 miles from the sea, every drive or bus journey becomes an opportunity to discover new landscapes. Around each bend lies the possibility of a hidden village green, a medieval church spire or a spectacular view that simply stops you in your tracks.

The following pages will guide you along some of the UK's most captivating routes, from the Causeway Coastal Route in Northern Ireland to the Malvern Hills along the border of England and Wales. They ask only that you slow down, look up from the sat nav, and remember that sometimes the most rewarding destinations are the ones you never expected to find.

So adjust your mirrors, lower the windows, and prepare to rediscover Britain from behind the wheel. The open road awaits. And it has stories to tell.

Shieldaig
North Coast 500 (p.168)

Wrynose Pass
Coniston Loop (p.150)

Garron Point
Causeway Coastal Route (p.174)

Winnats Pass
Bakewell to Castleton (p.144)

Llynnau Mymbyr
Llanberis Pass (p.162)

Ludlow
Malvern Hills (p.138)

Fishguard
Pembrokeshire Coast (p.156)

Clovelly
Atlantic Highway (p.122)

Durdle Door
Jurassic Coast (p.128)

Bliss Tweed Mill
North Cotswolds (p.134)

The Atlantic Highway, Barnstaple to Newquay

South West coastal classic

The 98-mile (158-km) journey along the Atlantic Highway (A39) from Barnstaple in Devon to Newquay in Cornwall is one of the most scenic coastal drives in England. After leaving the river-port market town of Barnstaple, the road passes the village of Westward Ho! with its 3-mile- (5km-) long beach, named after Charles Kingsley's novel of the same name. The writer Rudyard Kipling spent much of his childhood here and the first stanza of his poem

Above: Sea thrift along the Devon coastline near Westward Ho! on the Atlantic Highway.
Opposite: The village of Clovelly is famous for its steep, cobbled streets.

'If—' is set in stones along the promenade. The Isle of Lundy, 12 miles (19km) off the Devon coast and famous for its puffin colonies and other rare seabirds, can be seen on a clear day.

Quiet, winding lanes run parallel with the coast as it curves around the bay towards Titchberry along the Hartland stretch of Heritage Coast, which continues south towards Bude. Here the road passes the village of Clovelly, known for its steep, pedestrianised cobbled streets and impossibly picturesque harbour. Further west, at the lighthouse at Hartland Point, the coast makes a dramatic turn to the south towards Hartland Quay's old harbour area. Exposed to the prevailing south-westerly winds, the coastline here is notable for its high cliffs and shingle coves with a particularly dramatic stretch of the South West Coast Path (SWCP) running alongside.

Above: Hartland Point lighthouse marks the point where the Bristol Channel meets the Atlantic Ocean.

Opposite: The cantilevered bridge between the mainland and Castle Island recreates the original medieval crossing to Tintagel Castle.

Heading south, the road reaches Bude where the River Neet (a tributary of the River Stat) reaches the sea. Here the huge beach is a magnet for surfers, with the town being the home of the first Surf Life Saving Club, founded in 1953. Bude is also home to a seawater swimming pool carved into the rocks. Other popular locations along this section of the coastline include the expansive sandy beaches at Widemouth Bay and Crackington Haven, known for their folded sedimentary rock formations, which attract geology students from all over the country.

Not to be missed is Tintagel; the ruins of its medieval castle, steeped in Arthurian legend, are perched precariously between the mainland and the adjoining Castle Island. It is now connected by a modern cantilevered bridge, which recreates the route of the original historic crossing. Continuing the journey south, the road passes through the fishing village of Port Isaac, made famous by the TV series *Doc Martin*.

The road next passes through Padstow, known for its bustling harbour and culinary delights including Rick Stein's famous seafood restaurants. As

the journey continues, the sweeping sands of Watergate Bay emerge, attracting surfers and sun-worshippers alike. Finally, the route reaches Newquay, renowned for its vibrant surf culture and stunning Fistral Beach. Approaching the town, its expansive beaches come into view, framed by cliffs and the iconic Headland Hotel perched on the cliff's edge. The streets are always lively in summer, with surf shops, cafés and restaurants welcoming visitors from near and far. In winter, without the summer crowds, the town's cosy atmosphere and Cornish hospitality are even more in evidence while the weather varies from dramatic, stormy seas to crisp, sunny days. Newquay is also the perfect base for exploring other Cornish attractions, such as the Eden Project or the Lost Gardens of Heligan, which are also much quieter in winter.

Above: Famous as the surfing capital of the UK, the town of Newquay has 11 beaches.
Right: Boats moored along the harbour front at Padstow.

Jurassic Coast, Lyme Regis to Lulworth Cove

In the land of the dinosaurs

This meandering 45-mile (72.5-km) road journey along the south coast of England, between Lyme Regis and Lulworth Cove in Dorset, follows the central section of the Jurassic Coast. The latter is a UNESCO World Heritage Site and the only place on the planet where time's arrow has exposed 185 million years of Earth's geological history in the coastal cliffs, coves and beaches.

Lyme Regis, with its all-embracing 'Cobb' (harbour wall) and award-winning museum opened by Sir David Attenborough in 1999, was the home of Mary Anning, renowned for her discovery of a fossilised ichthyosaur skeleton in the early 19th century. To the east are its world-famous Blue Lias cliffs where she made many more of her discoveries. A few miles further east off the A35 is Charmouth Beach, studded with ammonites and belemnites that any keen-eyed

Left: Charmouth Beach on the Jurassic Coast is a rich source of fossils.

fossil hunter can find if they are sufficiently determined. Five miles (8km) further on are the towering cliffs of Golden Cap – the highest point on the south coast of England, at 627ft (191m).

Bridport and Weymouth follow as the coast road curves gently south-east. The former is a market town famous in centuries past for its ropemaking industry. In more recent times, it has become known for its thriving arts scene, galleries, local crafts and a lively Saturday market. Weymouth's esplanade has beautifully preserved Georgian houses, many of them now hotels and B&Bs offering accommodation in this popular seaside town. At its centre is the multi-coloured Jubilee Clock, built to commemorate the 50th year of Queen Victoria's reign in 1887. Beach-side entertainment during the summer months includes a traditional Punch and Judy show.

Left: West Bay, a dramatic shingle beach near Bridport, is part of the 'Golden Gateway to the Jurassic Coast'.
Above: The Jurassic Coaster bus service (shown here with Chesil Beach and the Isle of Portland beyond) runs between Lyme Regis and Poole.

If a detour appeals, south of Weymouth is Chesil Beach, a huge bank of shingle thrown up by the sea over many centuries that joins the mainland to the Isle of Portland. High up on Portland's summit, as well as some of the best views on the south coast of England, are the limestone quarries that produced the stones with which Sir Christopher Wren built St Paul's Cathedral.

Continuing east, the journey culminates at Lulworth Cove, famous for its near-circular bay, and adjacent Durdle Door where a giant limestone archway protrudes into the sea at the eastern end of its beach. Both are a must-see for anyone interested in geology; the sedimentary layers of folded rocks, laid down over countless millennia, each tell the story of a distinct chapter in Earth's history. In places these different strata have been pushed to near vertical by the movements of tectonic plates, the meaning of the term 'Jurassic Coast' spelt out in the history of the cliffs themselves.

These coves are not only geological wonders but are also alive during the summer months with wild flowers and butterflies, including the Lulworth skipper found only in this area. After the drive, there's the option to soak up the views further with a cliff-top walk between the two.

Left: Durdle Door, near Lulworth, is a giant limestone archway created by a combination of erosion and the movement of tectonic plates.

North Cotswolds Drive

Exploring the English heartlands

This scenic drive through a National Landscape (formerly Area of Outstanding Natural Beauty) crosses 25 miles (40km) of beautiful countryside in the north of the Cotswolds, connecting market towns and villages. The houses here are predominantly made from honey-coloured limestone with stone tile roofs and timber framing. Villages typically cluster around focal points such as parish churches, manor houses or market squares.

The journey starts in the market town of Chipping Norton, Oxfordshire, on the edge of the Cotswolds. Known locally as 'Chippy', the town was once a

Below: Bliss Tweed Mill, on the outskirts of Chipping Norton, was built in 1872. It has now been converted into luxury apartments.
Opposite: Bourton-on-the-Water on the River Windrush – the 'Venice of the Cotswolds'.

centre of the wool trade that brought prosperity to the region during the Middle Ages. Bliss Mill, a Victorian tweed mill with a distinctive chimney, is a landmark on the town's outskirts.

The first section to Stow-on-the-Wold follows the A44 and A436 through a landscape characterised by undulating hills and sheep-dotted fields divided by drystone walls. Stow is located at the meeting point of five major roads and was historically an important trading centre. At 800ft (244m) above sea level, it is also the highest town in the Cotswolds with panoramic views over the surrounding countryside. St Edward's Church, with its medieval tower, overlooks the location where the last battle of the Civil War was fought in 1646.

Heading south-west, you come to Bourton-on-the-Water, the 'Venice of the Cotswolds', which is spread out alongside the River Windrush that flows through its centre under a series of low stone bridges. The village green slopes down to the water flanked by limestone cottages, tea-rooms and cosy pubs. Popular attractions include a model village (a one-ninth-scale replica of Bourton itself), the Cotswold Motoring Museum and several traditional craft shops. The village can often be very busy, particularly at weekends during the summer months.

The final leg of the journey passes through the lesser known but highly atmospheric village of Guiting Power, with its Norman church and adjacent village green, on the slopes of a valley formed by a tributary of the River Windrush. From here, the road winds through Sudeley Castle's parkland approaching Winchcombe, with views opening up towards the Severn Vale and the distant Welsh mountains.

The journey ends in Winchcombe, once the capital of the kingdom of Mercia. This ancient Saxon town sits at the foot of the Cotswold escarpment, surrounded by beech woods and walking trails. Its narrow streets are lined with medieval and Tudor buildings, including several historic inns. Nearby Sudeley Castle, with its gardens and royal connections – Catherine Parr, Henry VIII's sixth wife, is buried in the chapel – makes for a suitably historic conclusion to this drive through the heartland of medieval England.

Above: St Michael and All Angels Church at Guiting Power.
Right: Stow-on-the-Wold is the highest of the Cotswolds towns with superb views over the surrounding countryside.

Malvern Hills, Welsh–English Border

History's highway

This spectacular 70-mile (113-km) road trip through the borderlands of Wales and England is like a journey back through the mists of time. It begins in Kerry, close to the source of the River Teme near Newtown in Powys. The Teme flows first through the Shropshire Hills and then the Malvern Hills, including the towns of Ludlow and Tenbury Wells, before joining the River Severn just south of Worcester. The River Teme was designated as a Site of Special Scientific Interest (SSSI) in 1996 in recognition of the rare plants and animal species that live in its waters and along its banks.

After first heading south-west to Knighton, travellers can take a stroll along Offa's Dyke, the 177-mile (285-km) earthwork traditionally thought to have been built by King Offa of Mercia in the 8th century to mark the boundary between Mercia and the various Welsh kingdoms (whether as a boundary marker or a defensive structure is disputed). An important wool-trading centre during the medieval era, Knighton once had two castles whose remains are now mostly well hidden behind constructions from more recent times.

Continuing east, the river valley reaches Bucknell and then Leintwardine, known to the Roman legions as Bravonium, an important settlement and supply depot along the route of today's Watling Street. Pressing on south through the Herefordshire countryside the road leads to Wigmore, dominated

Opposite top: Knighton Clock Tower was built in 1872 on the site of the old town hall.
Opposite bottom: The half-timbered frontage of the Feathers Hotel in Ludlow, Shropshire, was built in 1619.

by the ruins of its castle built on a limestone ridge. This was once the seat of the Mortimers, one of the most powerful families in the country during the 13th century.

A few miles to the south is Mortimer's Cross, where in 1461 the future Edward IV won a decisive victory that placed the House of York on the English throne. The battlefield, now peaceful farmland dotted with hedgerows, witnessed one of the bloodiest encounters of the Wars of the Roses.

Ludlow, a medieval walled town with perfectly preserved timber-framed buildings, is centred around its Norman castle perched on a sandstone cliff, with views across three counties. Beyond Ludlow, the valley opens into the fertile farmlands of south Shropshire. The road then passes through Burford, where a medieval bridge crosses the

Below: The Pump Rooms in the spa town of Tenbury Wells were built around the mineral spring in 1862.
Right: Burford House is an early Georgian house surrounded by a four-acre garden along the banks of the River Teme.

Teme. Tenbury Wells, whose history goes back to the Iron Age, was a popular Victorian spa town famous for its Pump Rooms, designed by James Cranston in the 1860s in Chinese Gothic style to house its mineral-water baths.

As the route enters Worcestershire, the landscape transforms once more. Here the Malvern Hills rise up over the Severn Plain, home of Great Witley whose baroque church contains one of the finest painted ceilings in the country. The approach to Worcester on the final leg of the journey passes through landscapes where cider 'hopyards' still flourish. The village of Martley is surrounded by orchards and farmland with St Peter's Church – an architectural gem – at its centre. Now the spire of Worcester Cathedral, with its multi-layered architecture dating back to 1084, rises into view as the Teme skirts around the south of the city before merging with the mighty River Severn.

Above: Great Witley Parish Church contains some of the finest painted ceilings in the country.

Right: Worcester, on the River Severn, with the Malvern Hills in the distance.

Remarkable Road Trips

Peak District Road, Bakewell to Castleton

Derbyshire eye-opener

For first-time visitors, this winding 25-mile (40-km) route from the market town of Bakewell to the historic village of Castleton is the perfect introduction to the Peak District. Along the way it passes many famous sites, including Ashford-in-the-Water with its 17th-century bridge, the 'plague village' of Eyam, the Chatsworth Estate, and the remote Hope Valley in the shadow of Mam Tor in the north.

It's a journey that illustrates the geological diversity of the Peak District, moving between the rolling hills of the White Peak around Bakewell and Chatsworth to the more dramatic landscapes approaching the Dark Peak near Castleton. Bakewell, home of the legendary Bakewell tart, is also famous for its medieval five-arched bridge crossing the River Wye, and the spectacular All Saints' Church, founded in the Saxon era, in the west of the town.

Right: All Saints' Church in Bakewell is a Grade I-listed building founded in AD 920.

Left: Medieval Sheepwash Bridge over the River Wye at Ashford-in-the-Water was once used for washing sheep before shearing.
Opposite below: The ruins of Peveril Castle, a Norman fortress perched on a limestone spur above the village of Castleton.
Below: The graveyard in the 'plague village' of Eyam.

From Bakewell the road winds north-west, following the River Wye upstream to Ashford-in-the-Water. This archetypal Derbyshire village is known for its limestone cottages and three historic bridges spanning the river. The Sheepwash Bridge, dating from the 17th century, was once used for washing sheep before shearing. Holy Trinity Church, the oldest parts of which date back to the 12th century, contains both Victorian stained-glass windows and a Norman stone arch featuring carvings of a wild boar. The tradition of well-dressing takes place in Ashford, with floral decorations displayed at the six wells around the village in late spring.

Heading east, the B6012 next reaches Chatsworth House, one of England's most magnificent stately homes; it has been home to the Devonshire family for nearly 500 years. Its art collection includes works by Rembrandt and Van Dyck, while the surrounding parkland was landscaped by Lancelot 'Capability' Brown. The famous Emperor Fountain projects water 290ft (88m) into the air, making it one of the highest gravity-fed fountains in the world.

Next stop on this journey through the history of England is the 'plague village' of Eyam. During the Great Plague in 1665, Rector William

Mompesson made the courageous decision to quarantine the village to prevent the epidemic's spread to nearby communities. The well-preserved Eyam Parish Church, where the rector delivered sermons during the plague, is a place of pilgrimage for many.

Approaching Castleton, the road winds through Hope Valley. This glacially carved valley forms a natural corridor between the limestone White Peak to the south and the darker gritstone of the Dark Peak to the north. Castleton itself is overlooked by Mam Tor and Peveril Castle, a Norman fortress perched on a limestone spur above the village. It was built by William Peveril, thought to have been the illegitimate son of William the Conqueror, around 1080. The village sits at the western end of Hope Valley and is famous for its show caves, including Blue John Cavern where the rare Blue John fluorite has been mined since the 18th century and is still mined in small quantities to this day. Castleton is also known for the dramatic scenery of the Winnats Pass limestone gorge, part of the National Trust's High Peak Estate.

Above: The village of Castleton on Peakshole Water at the western end of the Hope Valley in the Derbyshire Peak District.
Opposite: Winnats Pass is a limestone gorge in the National Trust's High Peak Estate.

Coniston Loop, Lake District

Three counties circular

This 48-mile (77-km) circular drive, of which there are a number of variations, is one of the Lake District's most memorable routes. Starting and finishing in the village of Coniston, it is made up of a combination of gentle valleys and remote villages connected by steep and winding roads between awe-inspiring fells and ancient woodlands. The village, overlooked by the towering peak of the Old Man of Coniston to the west, is located at the northern end of the eponymous lake. It was here on Coniston Water that Donald Campbell broke four World Water Speed Records in the 1950s.

Leaving Coniston, the road follows the A593 towards Skelwith Bridge before taking a left turn towards Wrynose Pass where the landscape rapidly

Remarkable Road Trips

Opposite: The village of Coniston with the Old Man of Coniston behind.
Below: Wrynose Pass, once used by Roman legions.
Bottom: The River Brathay flowing under Skelwith Bridge.

Above: Hardknott Roman Fort (Mediobogdum) looking out over Eskdale.

Opposite: Signpost showing the distance and direction to Rome and Roman-era sites in the area.

Remarkable Road Trips

transitions into rugged fell country. This ancient route, used by Roman legions and medieval packhorse trains, climbs steadily through a landscape of drystone walls and scattered farmsteads.

Wrynose Pass, with its 1-in-3 gradients and hairpin bends, demands respect. Cresting the summit, it's worth stopping to look at the Three Shire Stone, a limestone pillar marking the spot where the counties of Cumberland, Westmorland and Lancashire once met. The views from here are breathtaking, with the Langdale Pikes to the north and the Scafell range dominating the western horizon.

From here the road descends into the valley beside the River Brathay to Cockley Beck, where an old packhorse bridge crosses the River Esk. The road next crosses Hardknott Pass, another exciting but challenging road with the substantial remains of a Roman fort overlooking the valley. The views here are magnificent, encompassing the entire head of Eskdale and the surrounding peaks. The descent is as dramatic as the ascent. The valley opens up gradually, revealing the River Esk

Left: The shoreline where the River Esk meets the Irish Sea at Ravenglass.

Above: Birks Bridge over the River Duddon near Seathwaite, a favourite location of the poet William Wordsworth.

meandering through meadows dotted with sheep and ancient oak trees.

The road now follows the river through Eskdale Green to Ravenglass where the valley meets the Irish Sea. This small coastal village, once a Roman port called Glannoventa, sits at the confluence of three rivers: the Esk, Mite and Irt. The remains of the Roman bathhouse still stand, testament to the area's importance in ancient times. On clear days, the Isle of Man is visible on the horizon.

From Ravenglass, the route heads inland again, following the A595 south before turning left towards the Duddon Valley. The road through the valley is particularly beautiful, winding through the villages of Ulpha and Seathwaite with narrow lanes bordered by hawthorn hedges and stone walls. An open access area is located here adjacent to the road and the River Duddon, ideal for a picnic. The shallow, crystal-clear water with small pools and cascades is perfect for a paddle on a warm day, and there are fine views of the surrounding hills. William Wordsworth knew this valley intimately, penning a series of 34 sonnets dedicated to the River Duddon.

From here the road leads back to Coniston via Cockley Beck, turning right for a second drive over Wrynose Pass, this time in an easterly direction, before looping back to Coniston and closing the circle on a spectacular drive.

Pembrokeshire Coastal Drive

Beaches, bays, cliffs and a castle

This 180-mile (290-km) drive around the Pembrokeshire Coast, from St Dogmaels in the north to Amroth in the south, runs parallel to the Pembrokeshire Coast Path, passing through some of the most scenic landscapes in Wales, peppered with rugged cliffs, golden beaches and charming villages.

After leaving St Dogmaels and entering the Pembrokeshire Coast National Park, the road passes Poppit Sands, a wild but very popular sandy beach on the estuary of the River Teifi and the perfect opening scene for the drama that lies ahead. Heading west, the road drops towards Newport as the Preseli Hills loom above the fields to the south, each turn revealing more cliffs rising up out of the bay. This section, especially looking out towards Dinas Head, has some particularly impressive views.

Continuing towards Fishguard and Goodwick, the coastline never fails to disappoint, with Strumble Head, marking the southern border of Cardigan Bay, standing out as a highlight. The lighthouse on its rocky crag is always a dramatic sight, especially with the sun setting behind it on a summer's evening. Whitesands Bay follows, famous for its wide, sandy beach, thought by many to be the best surfing beach in Pembrokeshire.

Left: Newport, Pembrokeshire, looking south towards the Preseli Hills.
Above: The old harbour of Lower Town below the main town of Fishguard.

One of the highlights along this stretch of road is St David's Head, a promontory offering epic views of the rugged shoreline and, on clear days, glimpses of the distant hills of Ireland. After atmospheric St Davids, Britain's smallest city (population around 1,750), with its 12th-century cathedral, the road passes through the village of Solva whose magnificent winding harbour provides the perfect opportunity for a leisurely stroll and a chance to experience the local maritime culture.

Next comes St Brides Bay, framed by rugged cliffs standing sentinel over the changing moods of the Atlantic Ocean. Here the coastline is dotted with coves including Newgale, Broad Haven and Little Haven, each offering its own unique recipe of sandy beaches, rocky outcrops and

Left: St David's Head marks the divide between the Irish Sea and the Celtic Sea.
Above: Steep and winding hillsides surround Solva Harbour.

summer seaside vibe. The call of seabirds is ever present while the surrounding waters offer an excellent chance to spot seals and dolphins.

South of Milford Haven, the ruins of Pembroke Castle, the birthplace of Henry VII, stand imposingly above the adjacent river; further south, the coast road passes Bosherston and its famous lily ponds created in the 18th century by the Cawdor family. Heading east now along the south coast, the road passes beautiful Barafundle Bay and Freshwater East Beach with its surrounding nature reserve.

Finally the road reaches Tenby, famous for its Georgian architecture, sweeping beaches and buzzing harbour, providing a colourful glimpse into Pembrokeshire's rich maritime history. A few miles further along the coast is the village of Amroth – its long, sandy beach at the southern end of the Pembrokeshire Coast Path is a fitting end to the coastal splendour, historical richness and unique culture of this classic Welsh drive.

Left: Pembroke Castle, the birthplace of Henry VII.
Below: Tenby harbour bordered by colourful Georgian and Victorian houses.

Llanberis Pass, Eryri (Snowdonia) National Park

Mountain magic

The short, 3-mile (5-km) road journey through the Llanberis Pass in the heart of Eryri (Snowdonia) National Park is one of the most spectacular mountain drives in the UK. This ancient glacial valley forms a natural corridor between two of Wales's most striking mountain ranges: Yr Wyddfa (Snowdon) to the south and the Glyderau range to the north. Known as 'The Pass' in climbing circles, it is also one of the most famous rock climbing locations in the country. Worth driving in both directions for the full experience, the journey has some steep sections and limited options for parking en route.

Starting in the slate quarrying town of Llanberis beside Llyn Padarn, a ribbon lake formed by glacial action during the last Ice Age, the A4086 begins its steady climb into the mountains as the Dinorwig Slate Quarry becomes visible across the adjoining lake, Llyn Peris. The road winds upward alongside the River Nant Peris, through a landscape increasingly dominated by bare rock with ancient drystone walls lining the road.

The gradient increases noticeably as the pass proper begins. To the south, Cwm Glas and Cwm Dudlyn on Yr Wyddfa's north face are clearly visible as the Yr Wyddfa Horseshoe, including Crib Goch's knife-edge ridge, comes into view. The northern side of the pass reveals the Glyderau range, beginning with Elidir Fawr and followed by Glyder Fawr and Glyder Fach. The latter can be recognised by its boulder fields and rocky outcrops. However, its most

Opposite above: The slate quarrying town of Llanberis.
Opposite below: Dolbadarn Castle and Llyn Peris with Dinorwig slate quarry on the far bank.

famous feature is the Cantilever Stone on its summit, an apparently precariously balanced slab of rock that is in fact completely stable and has become a symbol of climbing in Eryri.

At the highest point on the route, Pen y Pass (1,178ft/359m), the mountain col has panoramic views in all directions. To the east is the Ogwen Valley and Mount Tryfan with its twin summit stones known as Adam and Eve. The car park at Pen y Pass is the starting point for several major mountain routes, including the Pyg Track and Miners' Track to Yr Wyddfa's summit.

The descent from Pen y Pass towards Capel Curig heads through a dramatic valley with steep sides and rocky outcrops interspersed with streams and waterfalls. As the road twists and turns, each new bend reveals a different view of the surrounding peaks. As Llyn Llydaw becomes visible in the valley below, its waters reflecting the crags, a gentler landscape begins to emerge in

Above: Rugged cliffs rising above the Nant Peris valley.
Opposite: The road snaking down from Pen y Pass to Capel Curig.

contrast to the mountain environment. This descent is particularly stunning during autumn when the trees create a tapestry of reds, oranges and yellows.

The route ends in Capel Curig, which has epic views of the Moel Siabod mountain and is home to Plas y Brenin, a National Outdoor Centre that runs courses in just about every conceivable outdoor activity. Walking, climbing, mountaineering, mountain biking and many other outdoor pursuits are

catered for. Nearby are an army training camp, a camp site, several cafés and hotels, and shops selling outdoor equipment.

Above: Llynnau Mymbyr lakes near Capel Curig, looking west towards Pen y Pass.

Remarkable Road Trips

The North Coast 500, Wester Ross Section

Scotland's Route 66

Launched in 2015 and often referred to as Scotland's answer to America's Route 66, the North Coast 500 is a circular road epic that follows the north coast of Scotland for 516 miles (830km), starting and ending at Inverness Castle. The Wester Ross section is one of the most scenic stretches of the route, with this 135-mile (220-km) drive boasting some of the best views in

Above: Loch Carron from the village of Lochcarron.
Opposite: View from the top of the Applecross Pass at Bealach na Bà.

Britain. Starting in Lochcarron, it follows the coast road to Shieldaig before heading east to Kinlochewe and north-west to Gairloch. It then runs parallel with the coast once more, followed by a short inland jump to Braemore Junction. The final section leads north to Ullapool.

From the village of Lochcarron, known for its weaving heritage and traditional crafts, the road heads west through a landscape of steep, forested hills and narrow passes. These slowly open out onto landscapes dotted with small stone cottages, with a backdrop of lochs and mountains. The high pass of Bealach na Bà has some particularly spectacular views. Along the coast to the west, the village of Applecross looks out towards the Isle of Raasay and the Isle of Skye beyond. Further round the coast, Shieldaig, on the banks of a sea loch, is an atmospheric fishing village looking out over the Torridon Hills.

Above: View from the A896 near Shieldaig looking towards the Torridon Hills.
Right: Dusk over the harbour at Shieldaig.

Heading east from Shieldaig, the village of Kinlochewe is the gateway to the remote wilderness of the Beinn Eighe National Nature Reserve; here the wilderness changes from dense woodland to open moorland and passes through Glen Torridon, surrounded by mountain peaks. As the route bends north-west to the harbour town of Gairloch, the coast comes into view with the turquoise waters of the Minch and the distant outlines of the Outer Hebrides providing some memorable views. As the road unravels, it skirts the edges of the west coast following a series of twists and turns that hug the cliffs with glimpses of secluded coves and views over often deserted sandy beaches.

The journey continues along the coast road, meandering through remote settlements bordered by the waters of the Atlantic Ocean. Seals may be seen basking on the rocks or slipping silently through the waves. In the skies above, sea eagles and ospreys soar through the air in search of prey. As the road approaches Braemore Junction, the dramatic peaks of An Teallach loom in the distance. From here, the narrow road, flanked by dense forest and open moorland, shadows the edge of Loch Broom.

Now the terrain becomes increasingly dramatic, the road skirting steep

hillsides before gradually descending into the coastal town of Ullapool. The drive finishes on the shores of Loch Broom, where whitewashed cottages and a busy harbour are framed against a backdrop of hills rising steeply from the water's edge.

Opposite: View of Loch Maree from Glen Docherty, close to the village of Kinlochewe.
Above: Journey's end – Ullapool on the shores of Loch Broom.

Causeway Coastal Route, Northern Ireland

In the footsteps of giants

Belfast to Derry/Londonderry: 120 miles (190km) along one of the most beautiful roads in the UK. Ancient castles, epic landscapes, villages lost in time, the restless ocean and the footsteps of giants. And for anyone with even half an ear for recent history, a road journey between these two great cities along the edge of the North Atlantic offers an exploration into the soul of Northern Ireland.

Emerging from Belfast and, after passing through Carrickfergus, and the busy port town of Larne, the road runs alongside the Antrim Plateau, part of the Antrim Coast and Glens National Landscape (formerly Area of Outstanding Natural Beauty), where rapidly flowing rivers run east and north-east into the sea. The coast here has a hypnotic quality as the smell of the salt-tinged breeze and the sound of waves crashing against the rocky shores below weave their magic spell.

Beauty spots along the way include remote

Right: The Black Arc tunnel near Larne.

Above: Cliffs at Garron Point near Antrim.
Opposite: The Carrick-a-Rede rope bridge at sunrise.

Murlough Bay, surrounded by rugged cliffs, with views over the Irish Sea to Rathlin Island and Scotland's Mull of Kintyre beyond.

The road continues towards Ballycastle, a harbour town on the north-eastern tip of Ireland, roughly halfway along the route and a firm favourite on Best Places to Live lists. One of the marvels on this magical road journey is the Carrick-a-Rede rope bridge. Suspended almost 100ft (30m) above the Atlantic Ocean, with puffins and razorbills soaring overhead, it connects the mainland with the tiny island of Carrickarede and was first assembled by salmon fishermen in 1755. It is now in the care of the National Trust. Although safety considerations have made it a lot less daunting, it is still a test of courage for anyone who dares cross it. Nonetheless, pre-booking is advised, so popular has it become.

Remarkable Road Trips

Next comes enchanting Ballintoy Harbour, a favourite film location (*Game of Thrones*), followed by the ruins of historic Dunseverick Castle, an ancient royal fort built on a steep-sided basalt stack.

Next on the list is the geological phenomenon of around 40,000 interlocking hexagonal basalt columns rising out of the ocean, the remnants of aeons-old volcanic activity. The alternative view is that Fionn mac Cumhaill, or Finn McCool, built his Giant's Causeway as a bridge over the sea to fight his Scottish rival, Benandonner. Further along the coast, Dunluce Castle emerges on the edge of a dramatic basalt outcrop. The castle's ruins have a haunting quality that charms visitors back into a half-historical, half-imaginary world of chivalry and conflict. It comes as no surprise to discover that the castle is said to have inspired C.S. Lewis's Cair Paravel, the capital of Narnia in *The Lion, the Witch and the Wardrobe*.

Heading westwards once more, the road passes Portrush and Portstewart, two very different coastal towns: the former is a destination for surfers, and the latter more sedate with its golf

Above left: Dunluce Castle, which is said to have inspired C.S. Lewis's Cair Paravel, the capital of Narnia.

Above right: The Giant's Causeway is made up of around 40,000 hexagonal basalt columns.

courses and tearooms. They are connected by a coastline of long, sandy beaches, coves and windswept cliffs.

As the journey approaches its final stretch, the landscape transforms once more. Time slows and the stone villages, walls weathered over the centuries, seem to be telling tales of resilience and endurance, conveying an innate sense of history and community. As the road winds closer to Derry/Londonderry with its medieval walls, the River Foyle comes into view, always a stirring sight in the waning sunlight of a summer's evening, signalling the final approach to journey's end.

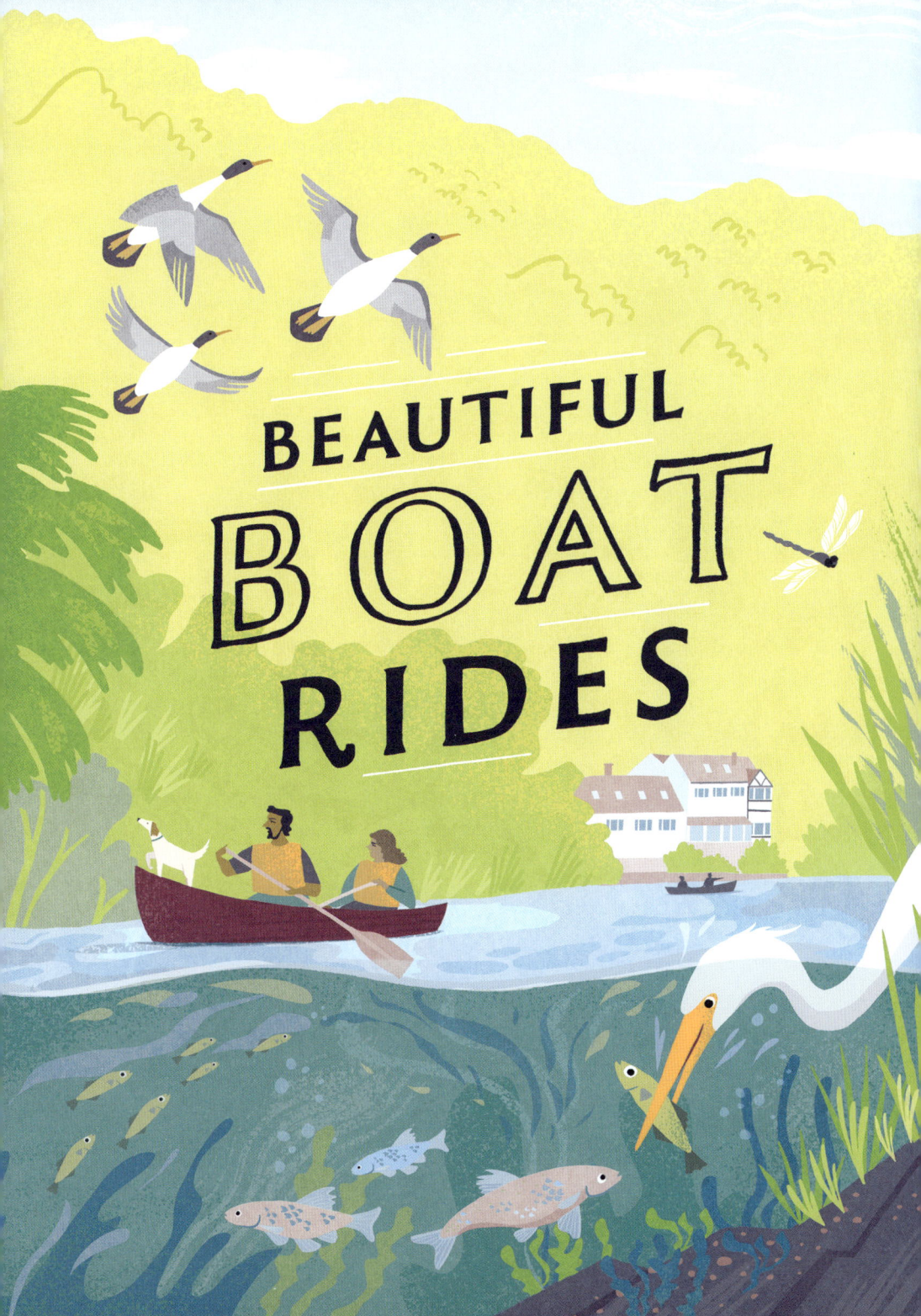

Beautiful Boat Rides

Long before the railways and the motorways, Britain's rivers and canals were the arteries of the nation. These waterways tell a story that flows through history. The Thames, which once witnessed Roman galleys and Tudor pageantry, now carries pleasure boats past the Tower of London and beside the dreaming spires of Oxford.

The variety of Britain's waterways is remarkable, and each has its own character and story. The Leeds and Liverpool Canal climbs through the famous Bingley Five Rise Locks, a staircase of five consecutive locks that lift boats 59ft in just 320 yards, while the Norfolk Broads spread out like an inland sea where medieval peat digging has created a unique landscape of reed beds and broad horizons.

From cross-country adventures to gentle river meanders, the following pages include some of Britain's most rewarding water journeys.

Loch Oich
Caledonian Canal (p.228)

Falkirk
Forth and Clyde Canal (p.224)

Bunbury
Shropshire Union Canal (p.204)

Ambleside
Lake Windermere (p.214)

Ross-on-Wye
River Wye (p.218)

Skipton
Leeds and Liverpool Canal (p.208)

Bradford-on-Avon
Kennet and Avon Canal (p.190)

Dittisham
Dart River (p.184)

Henley-on-Thames
River Thames (p.194)

St Benet's Abbey
Norfolk Broads (p.200)

Dart River Cruise, Devon

Agatha Christie's home from home

The River Dart in South Devon winds for 47 miles (75km) from its source on Dartmoor to the Dartmouth Estuary. The river is recognised for its biodiversity and is home to both Atlantic salmon and brown trout. Otters are also sometimes sighted, along with seals and kingfishers. The town of Dartmouth itself is the primary departure point for cruises. Located within the South Devon National Landscape (formerly Area of Outstanding Natural Beauty) with a busy waterfront and medieval castle – actually an artillery fort designed to protect the harbour against enemy shipping – the town is famous for its historic streets and Georgian architecture.

From here, commercial cruise boats sail upstream as far as Totnes and back, a journey taking 90 minutes each way, while individual sail and motorboats are also available for hire. On the opposite bank of the river is Kingswear, also protected by a castle. An iron chain once hung between the two fortifications, blocking enemy

Left: View of Kingswear seen from Dartmouth over the River Dart.

ships from passing. Kingswear is known for its steep, narrow streets lined with colourful thatched cottages and is home to the Dart Valley Railway offering steam train rides through the countryside.

The next landmark along the way is the Britannia Royal Naval College. Since 1863, Dartmouth and the River Dart have been the home of naval officer training in the UK. Today, it is the only remaining naval college in the country. The college's Edwardian architecture was designed by

Sir Aston Webb; its stately facade, featuring intricate stonework and elegant towers, is a spectacular sight in itself and dominates the waterfront.

The journey continues past Dittisham. Known locally as 'Ditsum', the village has many well-preserved historic buildings, including the 14th-century St George's Church whose tower has been a landmark for sailors for centuries. The village's winding streets are lined with thatched cottages dating back to the 16th and 17th centuries, their walls constructed with traditional Devon cob.

For many, the highlight of the cruise is reaching Greenway Quay and the Greenway Estate, summer home of the writer Agatha Christie, on the east bank of the river opposite Dittisham. The estate's woodland garden stretches down to the river's edge. The house's interiors summon up the atmosphere of a bygone era; it is easy to imagine Christie herself sitting by the window, lost in thought as she penned her latest story. Christie described Greenway as 'the loveliest place in the world' and treasured it as a holiday home for her family. Together, they filled it with

Above: Dartmouth Naval College on the banks of the River Dart.

Above right: The village of Dittisham, which stands opposite the Greenway Estate.

personal memorabilia from their travels and extensive collections brought to Greenway from Ashfield, Christie's childhood home in Torquay. The Georgian house and estate at Greenway is now in the care of the National Trust.

Finally, Totnes Castle comes into view. Perched imposingly on a hill, the Norman motte-and-bailey castle sits on a grass-covered mound in contrast to its ancient stone facade. Thought to have been built by Juhel, a commander in William the Conqueror's army, the castle was originally an earthwork and timber construction. A short distance further along the river is Dartington Hall, with its architecture dating back to the late 14th century and combining both Gothic and Tudor influences. Originally built for John Holland, Duke of Exeter, today it serves as a hub for culture, education and entertainment.

Above: Totnes Bridge over the River Dart.
Right: The house and grounds of Greenway, the holiday home of Agatha Christie.

Kennet and Avon Canal, Bath to Bradford-on-Avon

Riding the river train

Completed in 1810 and connecting Reading with Bristol by creating a link between the River Thames and the River Avon, the 87-mile (140-km) Kennet and Avon Canal was built to move coal, stone and agricultural products during the Industrial Revolution. It was one of the last great canal projects before railways transformed British transport. The journey along the canal from Bath to Bradford-on-Avon is 7.5 miles (12km) and typically takes 4–6 hours, making it an ideal day trip through the Avon valley's limestone landscape. Narrowboat day hire and short-break hire are available from a number of local operators.

The journey starts at Bath's Sydney Wharf where the canal is surrounded by Georgian architecture; Bath Abbey peeks above the skyline and ornate honey-coloured stone bridges cross the waterway, with willow trees brushing the water's surface. The first challenge presents itself immediately: Bath Deep Lock, one of the deepest locks on the entire UK canal system at nearly 20ft (6m). Deep Lock negotiated, the canal curves eastwards through Bath's Georgian terraces and passes Sydney Gardens, a public park dating back to the 18th century and a favourite of Jane Austen.

Leaving Bath's outskirts, it follows the contours of the Avon valley before giving way to open countryside. Approximately 2 miles (3km) outside Bath is the Dundas Aqueduct, an elegant stone structure carrying the canal 60ft (18m)

Opposite above: The Kennet and Avon Canal passes through the city of Bath.
Opposite below: The locks at Widcombe connect the upper level of the Kennet and Avon Canal to the River Avon.

above the River Avon. The aqueduct spans 150ft (46m) and features Doric columns constructed from local Bath stone. Its spectacular views look out over the Limpley Stoke Valley, with wooded hillsides rising on both sides. The sensation of floating high above the countryside while enclosed by the aqueduct's stone parapets is one of the canal's unique experiences.

The valley's limestone bedrock is surrounded by steep wooded slopes that rise directly from the water's edge. In spring bluebells and wild garlic line the

Left: Sydney Gardens, a favourite of Jane Austen, were opened in 1795.

Below: Dundas Aqueduct carries the canal over the River Avon.

Opposite: The canal basin at Bradford-on-Avon.

hillsides, while ancient beech and oak trees create a green canopy overhead during the summer months. The canal builders followed the valley's natural curves and due to the network of local roads, several bridges cross the canal at this point, including the elegant Dry Arch Bridge that carries a former railway line high overhead.

Approaching the market town of Bradford-on-Avon with its famous medieval bridge, the canal passes fields lined with drystone walls made from local limestone. The distinctive pale stone that characterises the area becomes more obvious as buildings begin to appear, quarried from nearby hillsides over many centuries. Eventually, the town emerges from behind the trees bordering the canal to reveal a first view of its famous bridge, with the building above its arches that originally served as a chapel.

The 14th-century monastic tithe barn, one of England's largest and best-preserved examples, soon comes into view across the fields. It was originally built to serve Barton Grange, a manor farm that belonged to Shaftesbury Abbey, the richest nunnery in medieval England. Bradford-on-Avon marks the journey's end as boats enter a lock that raises them 7ft (2m) to join the town's canal basin.

Beautiful Boat Rides

River Thames Boat Journey, London to Oxford

Big Ben to Folly Bridge

The River Thames winds through the heart of England for 215 miles (346km) from its source in Gloucestershire to the North Sea, and perhaps nowhere captures the essence of both England's history and its countryside more completely than the stretch between London and Oxford. This upstream journey of approximately 55 miles (88km) transforms from the busy urban waterway of the capital to the peaceful rural meanderings of Oxfordshire. Narrowboats can be hired to make the journey over a number of days from non-tidal areas of the Thames starting at Hampton Court, or shorter day cruises can be combined starting at Westminster Pier and stopping off at numerous locations along the way, including Richmond, Windsor, Henley-on-Thames and Reading.

As the boat departs from Westminster Pier in the heart of London, many of the city's most famous views are on display: down-river are the

Left: The Elizabeth Tower at Westminster Pier, known to most as Big Ben.

dome of St Paul's Cathedral, the Tower of London with, at its centre, the White Tower built by William the Conqueror, and the Gothic Revival towers of Tower Bridge; ahead are the London Eye and the Houses of Parliament with the Elizabeth Tower containing the great bell known as Big Ben.

After Battersea Power Station, now a luxury development, the boat passes under Hammersmith Bridge, with its ornate Victorian ironwork painted in green and gold, before passing through affluent neighbourhoods including Barnes and Mortlake, where rowing clubs line the banks. This section of the Thames hosts the famous Oxford and Cambridge Boat Race. Further on, Kew Gardens appear on the southern bank, the iconic pagoda visible through the trees.

Richmond Bridge, built in 1777, is one of the oldest surviving Thames bridges and the riverside at Richmond Green bustles with activity as pleasure

boats, kayakers and swans share the water. Continuing westward, the river passes Hampton Court Palace, Henry VIII's magnificent Tudor residence with its distinctive red-brick chimneys and formal gardens. The river then winds through Molesey and Walton-on-Thames, where the waterway narrows considerably and lock systems become more frequent.

    As the boat passes through Chertsey and Staines, the landscape transforms dramatically. The urban surroundings give way to water meadows, ancient woodlands and traditional English countryside. The river becomes more intimate, winding between overhanging willows. Windsor Castle dominates the skyline near Eton, its Round Tower visible for miles across the flat Thames Valley. Eton College's historic buildings cluster near the river,

Above: The Round Tower of Windsor Castle overlooking the Thames.

their brick and stone architecture representing centuries of English public school tradition.

Marlow follows, with its famous suspension bridge spanning the river and The Compleat Angler hotel overlooking the weir. Henley-on-Thames represents the social heart of the river, hosting the famous Royal Regatta each summer. The final stretch towards Oxford takes the boat through increasingly rural landscapes. Goring Gap cuts through the Chiltern Hills, where the river narrows between wooded slopes with ancient beech forests on the hills on either side. Abingdon's historic buildings include the ruins of its medieval abbey.

The journey concludes as the boat reaches Oxford, where the Thames is known locally as the Isis. Ancient Folly Bridge provides a fitting conclusion to a magical journey. Beyond it Christ Church Meadow borders the river, with views of the 'dreaming spires' for which the city is so famous.

Above: The Head of the River pub next to Folly Bridge in Oxford.
Right: The Angel on the Bridge pub, Henley-on-Thames.

Beautiful Boat Rides

River Bure, Norfolk Broads

Medieval meanderings

The Norfolk Broads cover 125 miles (200km) of waterways in the counties of Norfolk and Suffolk in East Anglia. Together they form Britain's largest protected wetland, made up of a maze of rivers and more than 60 lakes created by medieval peat digging. The history of the Broads is reflected in the historic windmills, drainage mills and thatched cottages that can be seen along the banks. Boats navigating the waters include traditional Norfolk

Broads cruisers with their distinctive high superstructures, modern motor cruisers and the occasional restored wherry with a black sail.

The River Bure (pronounced 'Burr') is one of the main arteries through the Broads. It flows through Wroxham, often referred to as the 'Capital of the Broads', where this 15-mile (24-km) round-trip to Ranworth Broad begins and ends. Busy marinas line Wroxham's riverbanks and boats of all sizes can be hired by the hour. The boats are easy to handle and designed for novice boaters, with speeds limited to 6mph (10kph) to protect the riverbanks and wildlife.

The wildlife of the Broads is one of its main attractions: herons stand motionless in the shallows; kingfishers flash past in brilliant blue streaks; swans glide along with their cygnets. In the background, the hum of

Below: View from Wroxham Bridge in Hoveton.

Beautiful Boat Rides

dragonflies, the calls of terns and the distinctive booming of a bittern can often be heard, while marsh harriers circle overhead during late summer. White-tailed sea eagles are also increasingly seen during spring and summer.

Heading upstream from Wroxham, boats pass Hoveton before reaching Horning, about 30 minutes away. Here, Victorian and Edwardian houses line the riverbank, their lawns stretching down to private moorings. There is a traditional 'staithe' – a wooden quay constructed from Norfolk oak – near the village that has served boaters for more than a century. Many boaters stop here for morning coffee at one of the riverside pubs or tearooms. Continuing along the Bure, the iconic St Benet's Abbey, a medieval ruin, rises into view.

Further upstream the landscape opens into classic Broads scenery with 8-feet- (2.5m-) high reed beds stretching to the horizon. Depth sounders show barely 3 feet (1m) in places, while ancient wooden posts, remnants of medieval peat workings, emerge from the water like skeletal fingers marking safe channels that local wherrymen have followed for centuries. Ranworth Broad, accessible via a short dyke, offers a perfect lunch stop. From the tower of Ranworth village church, known as the 'Cathedral of the Broads', there are glorious views over the nature reserve, while the floating thatched Broads Wildlife Centre provides fascinating insights into this unique ecosystem.

The return journey to Wroxham gives the surrounding landscape a different perspective as afternoon light transforms the water and reed beds. Back in Wroxham, you can explore the village shops and enjoy dinner at one of the riverside restaurants, while watching other boats return from their own adventures into the tantalising world of the Norfolk Broads.

Above: Horning on the River Bure.
Left: Sightings of great white egrets are increasing on the Broads.

Shropshire Union Canal, Chester to Nantwich

A Thomas Telford artwork

The Shropshire Union Canal was completed in 1835 as part of the vision of the great Victorian engineer Thomas Telford. Winding through the Cheshire countryside, it was built during the Industrial Revolution to carry coal, pottery and agricultural goods between the Midlands and the River Mersey. Joining Chester and Nantwich, this 28-mile (45-km) day trip has evolved into a recreational masterpiece in the modern era.

The journey begins with views of Chester's Roman walls on the eastern banks of the waterway. The canal here runs deep and straight before meeting the Chester flight of locks, a series of three chambers that lift boats gradually from the River Dee to the higher ground of rural Cheshire. The massive wooden gates, operated by traditional windlasses, require coordinated effort from the boat's crew. Water thunders through the lock gates as the chambers fill and empty – a process that takes approximately 20 minutes per lock.

Beyond the locks, the canal passes through farmland dotted with dairy herds and bordered by hedgerows. Telford's philosophy of following the natural contours of the countryside while maintaining the consistent depth and width of the canal is on display, with oak, ash and willow trees arching over the water, creating tunnels of green. At the village of Christleton, thatched cottages, Georgian houses and the 15th-century parish church of St James surround the canal. This stretch is also home to moorhens, coots and the occasional kingfisher, with pike lurking in the deeper waters.

Opposite above: Canal boats near Chester's city walls.
Opposite below: Bridge over the Shropshire Union Canal near Christleton.

At Waverton, the canal crosses the first of several aqueducts. The landscape gradually transitions from the undulating terrain near Chester to the flatter agricultural land of south Cheshire with fields bordered by red sandstone walls. One notable landmark along the way is the ruin of Beeston Castle, perched imposingly on a craggy hilltop. Built in the early 13th century, the castle was destroyed by Cromwell's forces during the English Civil War. The canal then passes to the north of Bunbury. Here, the tower of the 14th-century church of St Boniface can be glimpsed on the skyline with warehouses and wharves, once used for the transportation of cheese and agricultural products, lining the banks.

After passing between fields and clusters of trees, the Nantwich Canal Centre soon comes into view on the outskirts of this historic market town. Once busy with commercial traffic carrying salt from the local mines and finished goods from the potteries, it now serves as a mooring for pleasure craft and a starting point for exploring the centre of the town. The latter is now a conservation area lined with both Georgian architecture and half-timbered buildings from the Tudor era.

Below: Narrowboat moored on the Shropshire Union Canal at Nantwich.
Opposite: The Shropshire Union Canal with 13th-century Beeston Castle on its 350ft (107m) rocky crag.

Leeds and Liverpool Canal

Artery of the North

Built in the late 18th century during the Industrial Revolution, the 127-mile (204-km) Leeds and Liverpool Canal was a vital artery for transporting textiles, coal and other industrial goods between the two cities. It connected Lancashire's mills with global cotton markets and Yorkshire's wool trade with international buyers through the port of Liverpool. Passing through both urban and rural landscapes, the journey provides a cross section of the heritage of northern England.

Its many locks, bridges, aqueducts and tunnels demonstrate the engineering prowess of the canal's designers and builders, while the Pennine

Hills provide a dramatic backdrop with many stretches given conservation status. Regular sightings along the route include herons, the electric-blue flash of kingfishers, and water voles trailing ripples beside the banks.

At the start of the journey in Leeds, converted Victorian warehouses and cafés line the waterside as the urban landscape quickly gives way to the Yorkshire countryside. The famous Bingley Five Rise Locks follow – a staircase of consecutive locks that lift boats 59ft (18m) in just 320 yards (293m). On the way to Bingley, the canal passes through Saltaire, the Victorian model village built by philanthropist Titus Salt. This UNESCO World Heritage Site shows how the canal enabled industrial development in previously remote locations.

After passing the famous double-arched bridge at East Marton, the 'straight mile' is an elevated section of the canal on the approach to Skipton, the 'Gateway to the Yorkshire Dales'. Skipton Castle – one of

Opposite: Canal boats on the River Aire in Leeds city centre.
Below: Saltaire, the UNESCO World Heritage Site built by Titus Salt.

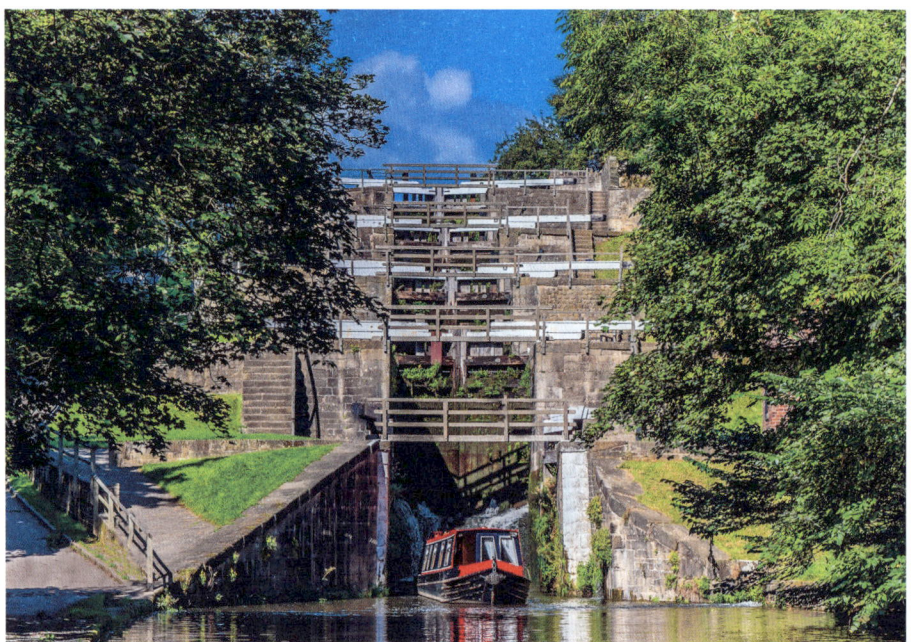

Above: Narrowboat exiting the Five Rise Locks on the Leeds and Liverpool canal at Bingley.
Opposite: The Thanet branch of the canal at Skipton, with Holy Trinity Church in the background.

the best-preserved medieval castles in England – overlooks the town from the limestone cliffs that rise above. Beyond Skipton, the moorland is criss-crossed by drystone walls and populated by grazing sheep. The towpath, worn smooth by horses pulling cargo boats in centuries past, is now popular with both walkers and cyclists.

Heading towards Burnley, the Foulridge Tunnel, stretching nearly a mile (1.5km) through solid rock, once required boats to be 'legged' through by men lying on their backs and pushing against the tunnel walls with their feet. Today's engine-powered craft navigate the darkness more easily, though it remains an adrenaline-pumping experience as boat lights pierce the underground gloom. As the canal descends gently into Lancashire, its character shifts noticeably. Industrial towns such as Burnley and Blackburn cluster around the waterway, their mill chimneys and terraced houses testament to the historical importance of cotton. A boom product of the Industrial Revolution, the raw material was grown by enslaved people in the

Beautiful Boat Rides

Americas, shipped in vast quantities to the factories of Lancashire and processed before being exported back across the globe.

Approaching Wigan Pier, immortalised by George Orwell's *The Road to Wigan Pier*, is Trencherfield Mill, a witness to the town's textile industry. Today's Wigan Pier is a recreation of the old coal loading point. On reaching the Mersey estuary, the Liverpool Canal Link passes the Museum of Liverpool and the M&S Bank Arena before reaching Liverpool's historic docks built to capitalise on growing trade with the American and Caribbean colonies. Here the skyline is dominated by the iconic 'Three Graces': the Royal Liver Building, the Cunard Building and the Port of Liverpool Building.

Opposite above: The entrance to the Foulridge Tunnel, which stretches for nearly a mile through solid rock.

Opposite below: A converted cotton warehouse at Wigan Pier.

Above: Narrowboat on the Liverpool Canal Link passing the 'Three Graces' and the modern Pier Head Ferry Terminal.

Boat Cruise on Lake Windermere, Cumbria

The heart of the Lake District

Lake Windermere is the largest natural lake in England. Many people would say it is also the most beautiful. At 10½ miles (17km) long and up to 1 mile (1.5km) wide, it was formed more than 13,000 years ago during the last Ice Age. There are many options for boat cruises on the lake, with everything from short 45-minute trips to longer 3-hour journeys from Lakeside in the far south, Bowness-on-Windermere and Brockhole on the east shore, and Ambleside at the northern end of the lake. Surrounded by hills and woodlands, the lake is dotted with small islands, and has been a source of inspiration for artists and writers, including William Wordsworth and Beatrix Potter, both of whom lived in the area.

A popular option for a cruise is the ride between Bowness-on-Windermere and Ambleside. Before leaving, the Windermere Jetty Museum, with its stories of boats and steam, just north of Bowness, is well worth a visit, giving an insight into Windermere's 200-year-old boating history and offering trips onto the lake aboard one of its

Beautiful Boat Rides

Above: Bowness on the eastern shore of Lake Windermere.

beautifully restored heritage boats. Shortly after leaving the harbour, views open out on the town's Victorian and Edwardian architecture, built during a period when the town was already a popular tourist destination.

Opposite the harbour is private Belle Isle, the largest of 18 islands on the lake and the only one that has ever been inhabited. During the Civil War it was a Royalist stronghold and today it is the location of a grand, circular house that was started in 1774. Wordsworth, however, was deeply unimpressed, describing the house as looking like a tea canister in a shop window.

Heading north, the shores are lined with clusters of woodland interspersed with stone cottages and Victorian-era houses. The lake is popular with both sailors and kayakers, and is also known for the many bird species that populate the shores and the hills around, including ospreys, peregrine falcons, buzzards and many waterbirds. There are also occasional sightings of otters. Landmarks that can be seen from the boat include Wray Castle, a Gothic Revival castle with

Above left: Wray Castle, a Gothic Revival castle cared for by the National Trust.

Above: Aerial view of Ambleside at the northern end of Lake Windermere.

distinctive turrets, towers and battlements, which was built in 1840 and has been in the care of the National Trust since 1929.

Arriving at Ambleside at the northern end of the lake, the spire of historic St Mary's Church rises above the rooftops behind the white-rendered buildings along the waterfront, which stand out like beacons against the traditional stone buildings lining its streets. A wide variety of small boats and yachts are moored in the harbour; they bob alongside historic wooden jetties, some dating back to the 19th century, backed by Victorian villas and traditional Lakeland cottages with walls built from local stone along the elegant sweep of the promenade. In the distance, the magnificent peaks of the Lake District rise in layered ridges, with Wansfell Pike and the Fairfield Horseshoe creating a surrounding amphitheatre.

River Wye Boat Journey

Going with the flow

At 155 miles (250km) from source to sea, the River Wye is the fourth longest river in the UK. It is also one of the country's most beautiful and ecologically important waterways. Starting as a stream in the Plynlimon range in the Cambrian Mountains of Mid Wales, it wends its way south-east to the Severn Estuary at Chepstow, forming part of the Welsh–English border along the way. It is home to a wide variety of wildlife, from Atlantic salmon to otters, mink,

Left: Chepstow Castle on the banks of the River Wye.
Below: Early autumn on the River Wye on the border between England and Wales.

Above: Aerial view of kayaks on the River Wye.

kingfishers and herons, while the bones of sabre-toothed cats and a mammoth have been found in and around the caves surrounding the valley.

The upper section of the river is characterised by its narrow banks and shallow, fast-flowing water; further downstream it widens out, making navigation easier and more enjoyable. Canoes and kayaks are popular choices due to their manoeuvrability in the sometimes shallow waters. Boats can be hired for everything from sunset trips to multiple-day tours, both guided and unguided. Cruise boats are also a popular option.

The different sections of the river all have their own charm and memorable features. At the north-eastern end, the 5-mile (8-km) stretch from the picturesque town of Glasbury to Hay-on-Wye – famous for its late-spring book festival – offers a delightful 2-hour paddle. The 14-mile (23-km) stretch from Ross-on-Wye to Symonds Yat is perfect for a day trip, and renowned for its spectacular scenery and the rapids at journey's end. Landmarks along the way include the stone arches of Kerne Bridge, built in the early 19th century on the site of a pre-Roman ford, and the nature reserve on towering Coppett Hill around which the river runs.

Symonds Yat Rock, at the top of limestone cliffs that loom over the river, is crowned with the remains of an Iron Age fort, now a Scheduled Ancient Monument. This internationally famous viewpoint is known as the 'Birthplace of British Tourism' after being popularised by the Reverend William Gilpin in the 18th century, who commented: 'If you have never navigated the Wye, you have seen nothing.' On the river below, the man-made rapids are a nationally important paddling site, run by British Canoeing and used for whitewater training and 'playboating' – a form of canoe freestyle.

Below: Ye Old Ferrie Inn at Symonds Yat was established in 1473.

Another popular section runs 5 miles (8km) between Monmouth and Whitebrook. Now gloriously tranquil, for more than a hundred years from 1607 the river drove waterwheels for mills – the remains of which are still visible on its banks – producing first wire and later paper. The paddle from Hoarwithy to Ross-on-Wye is also a popular route for both day trips and longer journeys.

The ruins of Goodrich and Chepstow Castles can both be seen from the river. However, at the southern end of the river it is the atmospheric ruins of Tintern Abbey – the former Cistercian monastery dissolved by Henry VIII and later immortalised in verse by William Wordsworth – which are the most popular spot for boat tours and sightseeing.

Below: View over the River Wye from Symonds Yat Rock.
Opposite: Tintern Abbey, the former Cistercian monastery dissolved by Henry VIII.

The Forth and Clyde Canal, Scottish Lowlands

The 'Canal Capital' of Scotland

The Forth and Clyde Canal is an historic waterway running coast to coast across the narrowest section of the Scottish Lowlands. Opened in 1790, abandoned in 1963 and restored in 2001, it was built to link Glasgow and the Firth of Clyde in the west with the Firth of Forth near Falkirk and Edinburgh in the east. Its primary purpose was to avoid cargo ships having to sail around the perilous north coast of Scotland. Along with its adjacent towpath for walkers and cyclists, these days it offers 35 miles (56km) – and 40 locks – of one of the most scenic boat journeys in Scotland.

The canal includes many impressive engineering and architectural creations along the way, including the Kelvin Aqueduct in the north of Glasgow as well as its swing and bascule bridges that open to allow taller boats to pass through. The canal roughly follows the line of the Antonine Wall, the ancient northern frontier of the Roman empire and now a UNESCO World Heritage Site, remnants of which can still be seen alongside the canal. Nature's offerings are equally spectacular,

Above: The Falkirk Wheel is a rotating boat lift that connects the Forth and Clyde Canal with the Union Canal.

Right: Bowling Harbour at the eastern end of the Forth and Clyde canal.

Far right: The Kelpies are 100ft (30m) horse-head sculptures inspired by the Clydesdale horses that once worked alongside the canals.

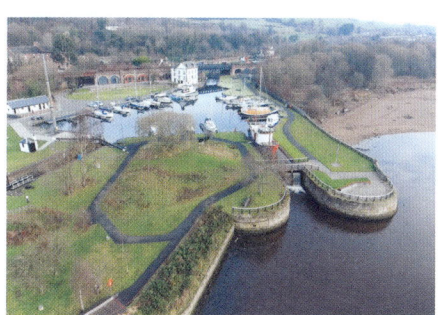

with impressive displays of wild flowers along its banks, and herons, swans, kingfishers, otters and water voles among its charismatic wildlife.

Due to the prevailing wind that blows from the south-west, most boat lovers travel west to east from the Clyde to the Forth. The journey begins at Bowling Harbour, a delightfully restored harbour village to the north-west of Glasgow where the canal meets the River Clyde on the west coast. Notable

Beautiful Boat Rides

Above: The rotating Falkirk Wheel, lifting narrow boats in the Forth and Clyde canal, is considered an engineering masterpiece.

views heading east include the historic Bowling Harbour itself, the Erskine Bridge, a cable-stayed box girder bridge crossing the River Clyde, and the Clydebank Titan Crane – the world's first electrically powered cantilever crane.

Emerging from Glasgow's eastern suburbs, the canal passes through Kirkintilloch – the 'Canal Capital of Scotland' – where the marina provides a quiet spot for a pause. On the 17-mile (27-km) eastward stretch towards Falkirk, the peace of the countryside prevails, with the route continuing under rustic bridges and through quiet towns and villages in the heart of Scotland. Here, remains of the Antonine Wall are visible alongside the canal, and the Auchinstarry Basin and its bustling marina are a popular stop.

Reaching Falkirk, excitement follows as boaters are greeted with the stunning sight of the Falkirk Wheel. Resembling a giant Ferris wheel, this is the world's only rotating boat lift, allowing boats to hurdle the 115-ft (35-m) height difference between the Forth and Clyde Canal and the Union Canal, which diverts towards Edinburgh. A few miles further east are the dazzling Kelpies – 100ft (30m) horse-head sculptures inspired by the Clydesdale horses that once worked alongside the canals. Lit up at night, they are a sight to behold.

It is now that the canal meets the peaceful waters of the River Carron, about a mile (1.6km) upstream from its confluence with the Firth of Forth at Grangemouth. The perfect end to an unforgettable journey across Scotland's central belt.

Caledonian Canal, Scottish Highlands

From the North Sea to the Atlantic

The Caledonian Canal cuts a dramatic 60-mile (96-km) diagonal slash across the Scottish Highlands, connecting the North Sea and the Atlantic between Inverness and Fort William. This journey traverses the Great Glen – the geological fault line that divides the Scottish Highlands and forms one of the most striking landscapes in the country. A chain of lochs – Loch Dochfour, Loch Ness, Loch Oich and Loch Lochy – connected by man-made channels makes up 22 miles (35km) of the total distance.

Completed in 1822, the canal is one of Thomas Telford's engineering masterpieces; it remains a vital link between Scotland's east and west coasts, serving both commercial traffic and recreational boating. There are 29 locks and 11 bridges along the waterway, and the entire journey typically takes between three and five days for recreational canal boats.

Left: Boat moored in the Clachnaharry Sea Lock – the eastern terminal of the Caledonian Canal.

Beautiful Boat Rides

Beautiful Boat Rides

Above: The ruins of Urquhart Castle on the north bank of Loch Ness.

Left: Fort Augustus: the canal's mid-point.

After travelling south-west along the canal from its eastern end, where the River Ness meets the Moray Firth, boats pass Dochgarroch at the head of Loch Ness. Next follow the romantic ruins of Urquhart Castle on the north bank where the loch gradually narrows. At Fort Augustus, the canal's mid-point, a staircase of five locks raises boats from Loch Ness to Loch Oich, the smallest of the three major lochs along the canal. Only 4 miles (6.5km) in length, it feels intimate and sheltered, surrounded by dense forests of Scots pine and birch, with gaps in the surrounding hills providing glimpses of distant peaks.

Next comes Loch Lochy, flanked by increasingly dramatic mountain terrain. This narrow loch stretches for 10 miles (16km) through the heart of the Great Glen, edged by steep-sided mountains particularly along the western shore where they rise steeply from the water. Dense forests carpet the lower slopes – a mixture of native Caledonian pine and planted spruce – with small burns cascading down the mountainsides through gaps in the trees.

The Nevis range soon becomes visible to the south-west, with the Grey Corries creating a dramatic backdrop. The canal now runs straight for 2 miles (3km), passing through farmland with clear views of Ben Nevis, which at 4,413ft (1,345m) is Britain's highest mountain. The final canal section begins at Gairlochy, where the boat enters the most engineered portion of the waterway.

The journey's final challenge comes at Banavie, 4 miles (6km) north of Fort William, where Neptune's Staircase – Britain's longest stair lock system – lowers vessels 64ft (20m) through eight consecutive locks. Each lock chamber is precisely calculated to manage the water flow from the Highland plateau to sea level. It's a process that normally takes about an hour and a half.

The journey concludes at Corpach Basin, where the canal meets Loch Linnhe and the waters of the Atlantic. The transformation from Highland loch to sea loch is immediate as tidal waters replace the fresh water of the canal system, and the landscape opens up to reveal the West Highland coastline. Fort William is located on the southern side of Loch Linnhe, accessible by road but separated from the canal terminus by the waters of the loch.

Below: Neptune's Staircase at Banavie is the longest staircase lock in Britain, lowering vessels 64ft (20m).

Right: Loch Oich in the central section of the Great Glen between Loch Ness and Loch Lochy.

Beautiful Boat Rides

Index

Note: page numbers in **bold** refer to information contained in captions.

Aberdovey 98–100
Aberlady Bay 95
Aberystwyth 98–102, **98**
Abingdon 198
Achnasheen 117
Adam and Eve (twin summit stones of Mount Tryfan) 164
Adlestrop 78, 80
Aidan, St 50
Aire, River 83, **209**
Alfred, Lord Tennyson 17
algae 20
   stonewort 39
All Saints' Church, Bakewell 144, **144**
Alnmouth **69**, **92**, 93
Alsh, Loch 117
Altnafeadh **59**
Ambleside 42, 45, **183**, 214, **216**, 217
ammonites 129–31
Amroth 156, 161
An Teallach 172
Angel on the Bridge **198**
Anning, Mary 129
Antonine Wall 224, 227
Antrim Coast and Glens 174
Antrim Plateau 174
Aonach Eagach ridge 59
Appleby-in-Westmorland 91
Applecross 170
Applecross Pass **168**
aquatic plants 20, 39
Areas of Outstanding Natural Beauty *see* National Landscapes
Arisaig 112
Arrochar Alps 111
Arthurian legend 125
Arthur's Seat 95
ash 26, 81, 204
Ashfield 188
Ashford-in-the-Water 144, 147, **147**
Asparagus Island 14
Atlantic Highway, Barnstaple to Newquay 121, 122–6, **122**
Atlantic Ocean 112, **124**, 159, 172, 176, 229, 232
   North 174
Attadale **69**, 117
Attenborough, Sir David 129
Auchinstarry Basin 227
Austen, Jane 190, **192**
Avon, River 190, **190**, 192, **192**
Avon valley 190
Awe, Loch 111

Bailey's Hill 18
Bakewell 121, 144–8, **144**
Ballintoy Harbour 178

Ballycastle 176
Banavie 231–2, **232**
Barafundle Bay 161
Barmouth **69**, 100, **100**
Barmouth Bridge 100
Barmouth Viaduct 98
Barnes 196
Barnstaple **69**, 70, 73, **73**
   to Newquay 122–6
Barton Grange 193
Bass Point 12, **17**
Bath 190–3, **190**
Bath Abbey 190
Bath Deep Lock 190
Battersea Power Station 196
Beachy Head 20, **23**
Bealach na Bà **168**, 170
Bearreraig Bay 64
Beauly Firth 114
Beddgelert 107
beech 26, 81, 136, 193, 198
Beeching cuts 87
Beeston Castle 206, **206**
Beinn Eighe National Nature Reserve 172
belemnites 129–31
Belfast 174
Belle Isle 216
Belle Tout Lighthouse **18**, 23, **23**
Ben Lomond 111
Ben Nevis 59, 112, 231
Ben Wyvis 117
Benandonner 178
Benedictine priory 50, **50**
Bentham Line, North Yorkshire Moors and Lancashire **69**, 82–5, **83**
Berwick Law 95
Berwick-upon-Tweed 93–5
Big Ben 195, **195**, 196
Bingley Five Rise Locks 182, 209, **210**
birch 231
   silver 61
bird's-foot trefoil 28
Birks Bridge **155**
Birling Gap **18**, 20, 23
Bishop, the (island) 14
bitterns 203
Black Arc tunnel 174
Black Mountains 26
blackbirds 80
Blackburn 213
Blackwater Reservoir 60–1
Blea Moor Tunnel **88**, 91
Bliss Tweed Mill 121, **134**, 135
Blue John Cavern 144
Blue Lias cliffs 129
Bluebell Railway, East Sussex **69**, 74–7, **74**, **77**
bluebells 50, 77, 80, 192–3
boat rides 6, 7, 181–232
Bodleian Library **78**
Boniface, St 72, 206
Borth 98, **98**

Bosherston 161
Bourton-on-the-Water **134**, 135
Bowling Harbour 224, 225, 227
Bowness-on-Windermere 214, **215**
Bradford-on-Avon **183**, 190–3, **192**
Braemore Junction 170, 172
Brass Point 18
Brathay, River **151**, 153
Bravonium 138
Brecon Beacons 31
Bridport 131, **131**
Bristol 190
Bristol Channel **124**
Britannia Royal Naval College 186, **187**
British Camp (Herefordshire Beacon) **11**, **31**, 33
British Canoeing 221
Broad Haven 159
Broads Wildlife Centre 203
Broadway Tower **11**, 24–8, **24**
Broadway village **24**, 26, 28
Brockhole 214
Broom, Loch 172, 173, **173**
Brown, Lancelot 'Capability' 26, 147
Buachaille Etive Mòr 59, **59**
Bucknell 138
Bude 124, 125
Bunbury **183**, 206
Bure, River 200–3, **203**
Burford (Shropshire) 140–2
Burford House **140**
Burnley 210, 213
butterflies
   Adonis blue 23, 28
   common blue 23
   Lulworth skipper 133
buzzards 17, 216
Bwlch Ciliau 56
Bwlch Coch 55
Bwlch Main 56

Caledonian Canal **183**, 229–32, **229**
Cambrian Coast Line, Aberystwyth to Pwllheli **69**, 98–102, **98**, **100**
Cambrian Mountains, Mid Wales 219
Campbell, Donald 150
canals 7
   Caledonian Canal **183**, 229–32, **229**
   Forth and Clyde Canal **183**, 224–7, **224**, 226
   Kennet and Avon Canal **183**, 190–3, **190**, **192**
   Leeds and Liverpool Canal 182, **183**, 208–13, **210**
   Shropshire Union Canal **183**, 204–6, **204**
Canna 112

Cantilever Stone 164
Capel Curig 164, **164**, 166, **167**
Caratacus 33
Cardigan Bay 98, 157
Carlisle 86
Carlisle station 91, **91**
Carrick-a-Rede 176, **176**
Carrickarede 176
Carrickfergus 174
Carron, Loch **168**
Carron, River 227
Castle Island **124**, 125
Castleton 121, 144–8, **147**, **148**
cats, sabre-toothed 220
cattle raiders 64
Causeway Coastal Route, Northern Ireland 120, **121**, 174–9
Cawdor family 161
Celtic Sea **159**
Cessford Castle 48
chalk 20
Charlbury **78**, 81
Charmouth Beach 129–31, **129**
Chase End Hill 33
Chatsworth Estate 144, 147
Chepstow 219
Chepstow Castle **219**, 222
cherry 80
Chertsey 197
Cheshire 204, 206
Chesil Beach **131**, 133
Chester
  Roman walls 204, **204**
  to Nantwich 204–6
Cheviot Hills 47, 48, **48**
chiffchaffs 50
Chiltern Hills 198
Chipping Norton ('Chippy') 134–5, **134**
Christ Church Meadow 198
Christianity 47, 48, 50, 72, 102, 222
Christie, Agatha 185, 187–8, **187**, **188**
Christleton 204, **204**
Church of St Thomas of Canterbury, Lapford 73
Cistercians 222, **222**
Clachnaharry Sea Lock **229**
Clan Campbell 111
Clapham 84
cliffs, Seven Sisters **11**, 18–23, **18**, **20**, **23**
'clints' (limestone pavement blocks) 38
Clogwyn station 107
Clovelly **121**, **122**, 124
Clyde, River 225, 227
Clydebank Titan Crane 227
Clydesdale horses **224**, 227
coal 17, 77, 87, 190, 204, 208, 213
coastal erosion 20, **133**
Coastguard Cottages 20
Cobbler, The 111
coccoliths 20
Cockley Beck 153, 155
Cold War 26

College Valley **48**
Colwall station 33
Compleat Angler hotel 198
Coniston 150, **151**, 155
Coniston Loop, Lake District **121**, 150–5
Coniston Water 150
coots 39, 204
Coppett Hill 221
Copplestone 72–3
Cornwall
  Kynance Cove **11**, **12**, **12**, **14**, **14**, 17
  Lizard Peninsula 7, 12–17
  Lizard Point **11**, 12–17, **14**
  The Atlantic Highway **121**, 122–6, **122**
Corpach 111
Corpach Basin 232
Corrour 111, 112
Cotswolds 10, 31
  Broadway Tower **11**, 24–8, **24**
  Cotswold Line, Oxford to Worcester **69**, 78–81, **78**
  North Cotswolds Drive **121**, 134–6, **136**
cotton industry 208, 213
Coventry, 6th Earl of 26
Coventry, Lady Barbara 26
cowslip 28
Crackington Haven 125
crane's-bill, bloody 17
Cranston, James 142
Crediton 72
Creedy, River 72
Cretaceous period 20
Crianlarich 111
Crib Goch **11**, 52–5, **52**, 107, 162
Criccieth 102
Cromwell, Oliver 206
Cuckmere Haven **11**, **18**, **20**, **20**, **23**
Cuckmere, River 23
Cuillin mountains 117
Cumberland 153
Cumbria 86
  Lake Windermere 40, 42, **42**, 45, **183**, 214–17, **215**, **216**
Cunard Building 213
curlews 50
Cuthbert, St **46**, 47, 48, 50
Cwm Dydlyn 162
Cwm Dyli 56
Cwm Glas 162

Dark Peak 144, 148
Dart, River **183**, 185–6, **185**, 187–8
Dart River Cruise, Devon 185–8
Dart Valley Railway 186
Dartington Hall 188
Dartmoor 72, 185
Dartmouth 185, **185**, 186
Dartmouth Estuary 185
Dee, River 91, 204
Dent 88
Dentdale 91
Derbyshire 147
Derbyshire Peak District **148**

Dere Street 47–8
Derry/Londonderry 174, 179
Devil's Staircase, West Highland Way **11**, 59–61, **59**, **61**
Devon 122–4, **122**
  Dart River Cruise 185–8
  North Devon Line (Tarka Line) 68, 70–3, **70**, **73**
Dinas Head 157
Dingwall 117
Dinorwig slate quarry 107, 162, **162**
dinosaurs 129
Dittisham **183**, 187, **187**
Dochfour, Loch 229
Dochgarroch 231
Dolbadarn Castle **162**
dolphins, bottlenose 98
Dorset, Jurassic Coast 7, **121**, 129–33, **129**, **131**
Dove Crag 41, **41**, 44
Dovey Junction 98
dragonflies 203
Drawing Room, the (cave) 14
dropwort 17
Dry Arch Bridge 193
Dryburgh Abbey 95
drystone walls 81, 87, 135, 153, 162, 193, 210
ducks, tufted 39
Duddon, River 155, **155**
Duddon Valley 155
Dumbarton Castle 109
Dundas Aqueduct 190–2, **192**
Dunluce Castle 178, **178**
Dunseverick Castle 178
Dunstanburgh Castle 93, **95**
Durdle Door **121**, **133**, **133**
Durham Cathedral 48
Dyfi, River 98

eagles
  golden 64
  sea 172, 203
  white-tailed sea 203
Earth's crust 20
East Anglia 198
East Coast Main Line, Newcastle to Edinburgh 7, **69**, 92–7
East Grinsted **77**
East Lothian 95
East Marton 209
East Sussex
  Bluebell Railway **69**, 74–7, **74**, **77**
  Seven Sisters **11**, 18–23, **18**, **20**, **23**
Eastbourne 18, 20, 23
Eden Project 126
Eden Valley 91
Edinburgh 7, 92–7, **96**, 224, 227
Edinburgh Castle 95
Edinburgh Waverley 93, **96**
Edward I 102, **102**
Edward IV 140
Edwardian period 186–7, 203, 216
Eggesford 73

235

egrets, great white 203
Eigg 112
Eildon Hills 47
Elgar, Sir Edward 30
Elidir Fawr 162
Elizabeth Tower **195**, 196
England 95
    see also Scotland–England border; Welsh–English border
English Channel **17**, 18
English Civil War 135, 206, 216
Erskine Bridge 109, 227
Eryri (Snowdonia) 98, 107, 164
Eryri (Snowdonia) National Park 99–100, 102
    Llanberis Pass **121**, 162–7
Esk, River 153, 153–5, **154**, 155
Eskdale **152**, 153
Eskdale Green 155
Eton College 197–8
Exe, River 72
Exeter 70
Exeter St David's station **70**, 72
Exmoor National Park 73
Eyam 144, 147–8, **147**

Fairbourne 100
Fairfield 41, 42, **42**
Fairfield Horseshoe, Lake District 7, **11**, 40–5, **41**, **45**, 217
fairy queen 34, **34**
Falkirk **183**, 224, 227
Falkirk Wheel **224**, **226**, 227
fault lines 33
Feathers Hotel, Ludlow **138**
ferns 36
field scabious 28
Finnan, River 112
First World War 78
Firth of Clyde 109, 224
Firth of Forth 95, 224, 227
Fishguard **121**, 157, **157**
Fistral Beach 126
Flagstaff Point 18
Flat Hill 18
fog signals 17
Folly Bridge 195, **198**, **198**
Forest of Bowland 83
Forestry Commission 73
Fort Augustus **231**, **231**
Fort William 59, 111, 112, 229, 231, 232
Forth and Clyde Canal, Scottish Lowlands **183**, 224–7, **224**, **226**
Forth Rail Bridge 95
fossils 129–31, **129**
Foulridge Tunnel 210–13, **213**
Foyle, River 179
Freshwater East Beach 161
fulmars 23, 98

Gairloch 170, 172
Gairlochy 231
Game of Thrones (TV series) 178
gannets 17
Gargrave 83

Garnedd Ugain (Crib-y-Ddysgl) 54–5
Garron Point **121**, **176**
Garsdale Viaduct (Dandry Mire Viaduct) **88**
Garve 117
Gateshead **92**
Gateshead Millennium Bridge **92**
Georgian period 26, 81, 85, 131, **140**, 161, **161**, 185, 188, 190, 204, 206
Giant's Causeway 178, **178**
Giggleswick 83
Gilpin, Reverend William 221
glacial meltwater 36, 38
Glannoventa 155
Glasbury 220
Glasgow 59, 224, 225, 227
    and the West Highland Line 109–12
Glasgow Queen Street station 109
Glaslyn 56
Glen Docherty **173**
Glen Torridon 172
Glencoe 59, **61**
Glenfinnan Viaduct, Scotland 69, 88, 109, 112, **113**
Gloucestershire 195
    Snowshill Manor 11, 26, 28
    Winchcombe 136
Glyder Fach 162
Glyder Fawr 162
Glyderau range 162
Golden Cap 131
Goodrich Castle 222
Goodwick 157
Gordale Scar **11**, 34, **36**, 38
Goring Gap 198
Grade I Scrambles **52**, 54–5
    see also Crib Goch ridge
Grangemouth 227
Grasmere 42
grasslands 30, 33
Great Glen 229, 231, **232**
Great Malvern 31
Great Marquess steam train **117**
Great Plague 147–8
Great Rigg 41, 42, **42**
Great Witley 142
Great Witley Parish Church **142**
grebes, great crested 39
Greenway Estate 187–8, **187**, **188**
Greenway Quay 187
Grey Corries 231
'grikes' (limestone pavement fissures) 38
Guiting Power 136, **136**
Gull Rock 14
Gullane 95
Gwynedd
    Snowdon Mountain Railway 56, **69**, 104–7, **104**, **107**
    Yr Wyddfa (Snowdon) Horseshoe 10, **11**, 52–6, **55**, 162

Hafod Eryri 107, **107**
Hammersmith Bridge 196
Hampton Court 195, 197
Hanborough 81
Hardknott Pass 153
Hardknott Roman Fort (Mediobogdum) **152**
Harlech 102
Harlech Castle 102, **102**
'Harry Potter Train' *see Jacobite, The* (steam train)
Hart Crag 41, 44
Hartland Devon Heritage Coast 124
Hartland Point 124, **124**
Hartland Quay 124
Haven Brow 18
hawthorn 80
Hay-on-Wye 220
Head of the River pub **198**
Headland Hotel 126
heather **14**, 87
Heligan, Lost Gardens of 126
Hellifield 83, **83**
Helvellyn 44
Henley-on-Thames **183**, 195, 198, **198**
Henry VII 161, **161**
Henry VIII 47, 136, 197, 222, **222**
Herefordshire 138–40
    Malvern Hills **11**, 30–3, **31**, 33
Heron Pike 41, 42, **42**
herons 73, 98, 199, 209, 220, 225
Hethpool 48, **48**
Heysham Power Station 85
High Bentham 84
High Peak Estate 148, **148**
High Pike **11**, 41, 45, **45**
Highlands 59, 60
Hill Barn Farm 28, **28**
hill forts **31**, 33, 47, 102
Hoarwithy 222
'Hogwarts Express' *see Jacobite, The* (steam train)
Holland, John, Duke of Exeter 188
Holy Trinity Church, Ashford-in-the-Water 147
Holy Trinity Church, Skipton 210
Honeybourne 81
Hope Valley 144, 148, **148**
Horning 203, **203**
Horsted Keynes **69**, 77
Horton-in-Ribblesdale 88
House of York 140
Houses of Parliament 196
Hoveton **199**, 203
hydroelectric plants 61

Ice Age 20, 36, 38, 162, 214
ichthyosaurs 129
igneous rocks 33
Industrial Revolution 7, 190, 204, 208
Ingleborough 83, 88

Inner Hebrides 63–4
Inverness 114, 229
Inverness Castle 168
Ireland 56, 107, 159
Irish Sea 6, 98, 104, **154**, 155, **159**, 176
Iron Age 142
Iron Age hill forts **31**, 33, 102, 221
Irt, River 155
Isle of Lundy 124
Isle of Man 56, 107, 155
Isle of Portland **131**, 133
Isle of Raasay 170
Isle of Skye 114, 117, 170
  Old Man of Storr and the Quiraing **11**, 63–4, **63**, **64**
Isle of Wight 17

Jacobite, The (steam train) 7, 109, **111**, **113**
Jacobite Rebellions 59
Janet's Foss 34, **34**, 36
Jedburgh Abbey 95
Jekyll, Gertrude 50
John, King 81
Jubilee Hill 31, 33
Juhel 188
Jurassic Coast, Dorset, Lyme Regis to Lulworth Cove 7, **121**, 129–33, **129**, **131**
Jurassic Coast bus services **131**

Keighley 83
Kelpies **224**, 227
Kelso 95
Kelso Abbey 95
Kelvin Aqueduct 224
Kennet and Avon Canal, Bath to Bradford-on-Avon **183**, 190–3, **190**, **192**
Kerne Bridge 220–1
Kerry 138
Kessock Bridge 114
Kew Gardens 196
Kilchurn Castle 111
Kilpatrick Hills 109
kingfishers 73, 185, 199, 204, 209, 220, 225
Kingham 81, **81**
Kingscote 77, **77**
Kingsley, Charles 122
Kingswear 185–6, **185**
Kinlochewe 170, 172, **172**
Kinlochleven 59, 60, **61**
Kipling, Rudyard 122–4
Kirk Yetholm 48, **48**
Kirkintilloch 227
kittiwakes 23
Knighton 138
Knighton Clock Tower **138**
Kyle of Lochalsh Line, Scottish Highlands **69**, 114–17, **114**, **117**
Kyleakin, Isle of Skye 114
Kynance Cove, Cornwall **11**, 12, **12**, 14, **14**, 17

Ladies' Bathing Pool, the (cave) 14
lady's bedstraw 17
Lake District 84, 85
  Coniston Loop **121**, 150–5
  Fairfield Horseshoe 7, **11**, 40–5, **41**, **45**, 217
  Lake Windermere 214–17
Lammermuir Hills 95
Lamvern Hills 81
Lancashire 153, 208, 213
  Bentham Line 82–5
Lancaster 83, 84–5
Lancaster Canal 84–5
Land's End 12
landslips 63
Langdale Pikes 153
Langland, William 30
Lapford 73
lapwings 50
Larne 174
lavender fields 28, **28**
Leathan, Loch 64
Leeds 83, 208–9, **209**
Leeds and Liverpool Canal 182, **183**, 208–13, **210**
  Thanet branch **210**
Leintwardine 138
Leven, Loch 60, **61**
Leven, River 61
Lewis, C.S., *The Lion, the Witch and the Wardrobe* 178
lifeboat stations 17
lighthouses
  Belle Tout **18**, 23, **23**
  Hartland Point **124**
  Lizard 17, **17**
limestone 34, **34**, 36, 38, 80–1, 83–4, 87, **133**, **133**, 134–5, 140, **147**, 148, **148**, 153, 190, 192, 210, 221
  pavements 38
Limpley Stoke Valley 192
Lindisfarne 47, 48, 50, **50**
Lindisfarne Castle **11**, 50, 93
Linnhe, Loch 232
Lion's Den 17
Little Haven 159
'Little North Western' *see* Bentham Line
Liverpool 209
Liverpool Canal Link 213, **213**
Lizard Lighthouse 17, **17**
Lizard Peninsula, Cornwall 7, 12–17
Lizard Point, Cornwall **11**, 12–17, **14**
Lizard village, Cornwall 17
Llanberis 162, **162**
Llanberis Pass, Eryri (Snowdonia) National Park **121**, 162–7
Llanberis station 104, 107
Llanberis valley **107**
Lloyd's Signal Station 17, **17**
Llwyngwril 100
Llydaw, Llyn **55**, 56, **56**, 107, 164

Llŷn Peninsula 102
Lochcarron village **168**, 170
Lochy, Loch 229, 231, **232**
Lomond, Loch 111
London 93
  boat journey from London to Oxford 195–8
London Eye 196
Long, Loch 109
Long Mynd 26
Lost Gardens of Heligan 126
Loughrigg **41**
Low Pike **41**, 45, **45**
Low Sweden Bridge 42
Lower Town **157**
Ludlow **121**, **138**, **138**, 140
Luguvalium 91
Lulworth Cove 129–33, **133**
Lune, River 84
Lune Valley 83
Lutyens, Sir Edwin 50
Lyme Regis 129–33, **131**

M&S Bank Area 213
mac Cumhaill, Fionn (Finn McCool) 178
Magna Carta 81
Malham Beck **34**, 36
Malham Cove, Yorkshire Dales **11**, 34–9, **36**
Malham Tarn 36, 39, **39**
Malham village 34, 36, 39
Mallaig, West Highland Line 109–12, **113**
Malvern Hills **11**, 30–3, **31**, 33, 120, **121**, **142**
  Welsh–English border 138–42
Malvern Water 31
Mam Tor 144, 148
Mamores 59, 60
mammoths 220
Marconi, Guglielmo 17
Maree, Loch **173**
Marlow 198
marsh harriers 203
Martello tower, Seaford 23
Martley 142
Mary, Queen of Scots 91
Mawddach Estuary 98, 100, **100**
McAlpine, Sir Robert 'Concrete Bob' 112
McGregor, Rob Roy 111
meadow pipits 50, 64
meadowsweet 78
Meall na Suiramach 63, 64
Melrose Abbey **46**, 47, 95
Mercia 136, 138
Mersey, River 204
Mersey estuary 213
metamorphic rocks 33
Midlands 204
Milford Haven 161
Minch 172
Miners' Track 56, **56**, 164
mink 220
Mite, River 155
Moel Siabod 166

237

Molesey 197
Mompesson, Rector William 147–8
Monessie Gorge 112
monks 48
Monmouth 222
moorhens 39, 204
Morar 112
Moray Firth 114, 231
Morecambe Bay 69, 83, 85, **85**
Moreton-in-Marsh 80, 81
Morpeth 93
Morris, William 26
Mortimer family 140
Mortimer's Cross 140
Mortlake 196
Muck 112
Mull of Kintyre 176
Murlough Bay (County Antrim) 176
Museum of Liverpool 213
Mymbyr, Llynnau **121**, **167**

Nab Scar 41, **41**, 42
Nant Peris valley **164**
Nantwich 204–6, **206**
Nantwich Canal Centre 206
Napoleonic era 23
narrowboats 190, 195, **206**, **210**, 213, 220, **226**
National Landscapes 24, 30, 80, 83, 134, 174, 185
Needle, the (rock formation) 64
Neet, River 125
Neptune's Staircase 231–2, **232**
Ness, Loch 229, 231, **231**, **232**
Ness, River 231
Nevis range 231
Newcastle 7, 92–7
Newcastle station 93
Newgale 159
Newport (Pembrokeshire) 157, **157**
Newquay 122, 126, **126**
 The Atlantic Highway 122–6
Newton St Cyres 72
Newtown (Powys) 138
Norfolk 198
Norfolk Broads 182, **183**
 River Bure 200–3
Norman architecture 136, 140, 147–8, **147**, 188
North Berwick 95
North Coast 500 route 7
 Wester Ross section **121**, 168–73
North Cotswolds Drive **121**, 134–6, **136**
North Devon 73
North Devon Line (Tarka Line) 68, 70–3, **70**, **73**
North Hill 31
North Malvern 31
North Pennines, Settle to Carlisle Railway 86–91
North Sea 7, 93, 114, 195, 229
North Yorkshire Moors 82–5

Northern Ireland 120
 Causeway Coastal Route 120, **121**, 174–9
Northumberland 10, 47
Northumbria 7, 93, **95**
 St Cuthbert's Way **11**, 47–50, **48**
nuclear bunkers 26

oak 26, 42, 72, 80, 104, 155, 193, 203, 204
Oban 111
Offa, King 138
Offa's Dyke 138
Ogwen Valley 164
Oich, Loch **183**, 229, 231, **232**
Old Man of Coniston 85, 150, **151**
Old Man of Storr and the Quiraing, Isle of Skye **11**, 63–4, **63**, **64**
Old Norse 64
Orwell, George 213
ospreys 98, 172, 216
otters 185, 216, 219, 225
Outer Hebrides 172
Oxford 78–81, **78**, 182, **198**
 boat journey from London to Oxford 195–8
Oxford and Cambridge Boat Race 196
Oxfordshire 134, 195

packhorse trains 153
Padarn, Llyn 162
Padstow 125, **126**
Pannier Market, Barnstaple 73
Parish Church of St Mary the Virgin, Lindisfarne 50
Parlour, the (cave) 14
Parr, Catherine 136
pasqueflower 28
Pass of Brander 111
Peak District Road, Bakewell to Castleton 144–8
Peakshole Water **148**
Pembroke Castle 161, **161**
Pembrokeshire Coast National Park 157
Pembrokeshire Coast Path 156, 161
Pembrokeshire Coastal Drive **121**, 156–61
Pen Olver 17
Pen-y-ghent 88
Pen y Pass 164, **164**, **167**
Pen y Pass car park **52**, 54, 56, 164
Pennine Way 36
Pennine Hills 83, 84, 87, 208–9
 North 86–91
peregrine falcons 17, 23, 216
Peris, Llyn 162, 164
Perseverance Hill 31
Peveril, William 148
Peveril Castle **147**, 148
Pier Head Ferry Terminal 213
pike 204

pilgrim pots 50
pilgrimage **46**, 47, 50, 148
pine, Caledonian 231
'plague village' (Eyam) 144, 147–8, **147**
plankton 20
Plantation Viaduct **114**
Plas y Brenin National Outdoor Centre 166–7
Pleiades 18
Plynlimon range 219
Polpeor Cove 17
Poole **131**
Poppit Sands 157
Port Isaac 125
Port of Liverpool Building 213
Porthmadog 102
Portrush 178–9
Portstewart 178–9
Potter, Beatrix 214
Pre-Raphaelites 26
Preseli Hills 157, **157**
primroses 28, 50
Prison, the (cliff) 64
puffins 50, 124, 176
Pump Rooms, Tenbury Wells 140, 142
Pwllheli 98–102
Pyg Track 54, **56**, 164

Quiraing, Isle of Skye **11**, 63–4, **63**

Radcliffe Camera **78**
radio experiments 17
Rannoch Moor 59, 111
Rannoch Viaduct **109**
Ranworth Broad 199, 203
Ranworth village church ('Cathedral of the Broads') 203
Rathlin Island 176
Ravenglass **154**, 155
ravens 17
razorbills 98, 176
Reading 190, 195
Ribble Valley **87**, 88
Ribblehead 88
Ribblehead Viaduct 69, **87**, 88
Richmond 195
Richmond Bridge 196–7
Richmond Green 196–7
River Nant Pass 162
road trips 6, 119–79
Rocky Valley 107
Roman bathhouses 155
Roman forts 155
Roman legions 138, **151**, 153
Roman roads 47–8, 138
Roman walls, Chester 204, **204**
Romans 33, 68, 91, **152**, 155, 182, 224
Ross-on-Wye **183**, 220, 222
Rothay, River 42
Rough Brow 18
Royal Border Bridge 95, **96**
Royal Liver Building 213
Royal Regatta (Henley) 198

Royalists, English Civil War 216
Rum (isle) 112
Rydal valley 41
Rydal Water **41**, **42**

St Ann's Well 31
St Barnabas Church, Snowshill 28, **28**
St Benet's Abbey **183**, 203
St Brides Bay 159
St Cuthbert's Cave 48
St Cuthbert's Cross **92**
St Cuthbert's Way, Northumbria 11, 47–50, **48**
St Davids 159
St David's Head 159, **159**
St Dogmaels 156, 157
St George's Church, Dittisham 187
St James' Church, Christleton 204
St Mary's Church, Ambleside 217
St Michael and All Angels Church, Guiting Power **136**
St Paul's Cathedral 133, 195–6
St Peter's Church, Martley 142
salmon, Atlantic 185, 219
Salt, Titus 209, **209**
Saltaire 209, **209**
Saxons 136, 144, **144**
Scafell range 153
Scheduled Ancient Monuments 221
Scotland 56, 88, 91, 92–7, 95, 176
   Kyle of Lochalsh Line 114–17, **114**, **117**
   North Coast 500 route 7, **121**, 168–73
   The Devil's Staircase **11**, 59–61, **59**, **61**
Scotland–England border 91, 95, **96**
Scots pine 60, 231
Scottish borders 7, 47, **48**, 93–5
Scottish Highlands 6, 10
   Caledonian Canal **183**, 229–32, **229**
   Kyle of Lochalsh Line **69**, 114–17, **114**, **117**
   West Highland Line 7, **69**, 109–12, **109**, **111**, **113**
   West Highland Way **11**, 59–61, **59**, **61**
Scottish Lowlands, Forth and Clyde Canal **183**, 224–7, **224**, **226**
Seaford 18, 20, 23
seals 17, 50, 98, 172, 185
Seathwaite 155, **155**
sedimentary rocks 63, **64**, 125, 133
selfheal 17
semaphore communications 17
serpentine 14
Settle **87**

Settle to Carlisle Railway, Yorkshire Dales and North Pennines 68, **69**, 86–91
Seven Sisters, East Sussex **11**, 18–23, **18**, **20**, **23**
Severn, River **81**, 138, 142, **142**
Severn Estuary 219
Severn Plain 142
Severn Vale 136
Severn Valley 31
Shaftesbury Abbey 193
sharks, basking 17
shearwaters 17
sheep 210
Sheepwash Bridge 147, **147**
Sheffield Park, East Sussex 74, **74**
Shenberrow Hill 28
Shieldaig **121**, 170, **170**, 172
Shipley 83
Short Brow 18
Shropshire Hills 138
Shropshire Union Canal **224**, 227
   Chester to Nantwich 6, **183**, 204–6, **204**, **206**
Sites of Special Scientific Interest (SSSIs) 39, **39**, 138
Skelwith Bridge 150, **151**
Skipton 83, **83**, **183**, 209–10, **210**
Skipton Castle 209–10
Skye Bridge 117
skylarks 50
Smailholm Tower 95
Snowdon Mountain Railway, Gwynedd 56, **69**, 104–7, **104**, **107**
Snowdon, Mt (Yr Wyddfa) 102, 162
   Snowdon (Yr Wyddfa) Horseshoe 10, **11**, 52–6, **55**, 162
Snowdonia (Eryri) 98, 107, 164
Snowdonia (Eryri) National Park 99–100, 102
   Llanberis Pass **121**, 162–7
Snowshill 28, **28**
Snowshill Manor **11**, **26**, **28**
Solva Harbour 159, **159**
Sound of Raasay 64
South Downs 10, 77
South Wales 26
South West Coast Path (SWCP) **12**, **124**
Spanish Armada 26
Special Area of Conversation (SAC) 39, **39**
spruce 231
squill 17
Staines 197
staithe 203
Stanier Class 8F steam locomotives 91
Stat, River 125
steam trains 74–7, 78–80, **83**, **88**, **91**, **100**, **100**, **117**, 186
Stein, Rick 125
stone trig points 56

stonechats 17
Storr Lookout Point 64
Stow-on-the-Wold 135, **136**
Strathcarron 117
Strathpeffer Valley 117
Stromeferry **114**
Strumble Head 157
Sudeley Castle 136
Suffolk 198
Sugarloaf 31
Summer Hill 31
Summit station 107
Surf Life Saving Club 125
swans 199, 225
Sydney Gardens 190, **192**
Sydney Wharf, Bath 190
Symonds Yat 220, **221**
Symonds Yat Rock 221, **222**

Table, the (rock formation) 64
Table Hill 31
Talyllyn steam railway 100, **100**
Tarka Line, Devon 68, **69**, 70–3, **70**, **73**
Tarka Walking Trail 70
Taw, River 70, 72, 73, **73**
teals 39
tectonic plates **133**
Teifi, River 157
Telford, Thomas 204, 229
Teme, River 138, **140**, 142
Tenbury Wells 138, **140**, 142
Tenby 161, **161**
terns 50, 203
Teyrn, Llyn 56, **56**, 107
Thames, River 182, 190
   boat journey from London to Oxford **183**, 195–8, **197**
Thames Valley 197
Thomas, Edward 78
'Three Graces' 213, **213**
Three Shire Stone 153
Tintagel 125
Tintagel Castle **124**
Tintern Abbey 222, **222**
Titchberry 124
Tolkien, J. R. R. 30, 38
Tonfanau 100
Tor Balk 14
Tornado steam locomotive **88**
Torquay 188
Torridon Hills **170**
Totnes 185
Totnes Bridge **188**
Totnes Castle 188
Tower Bridge 196
Tower of London 182, 196
train journeys 6, 7, 67–117
Treig, Loch 112
Tremadog Bay 102
Trencherfield Mill 213
Trotternish Peninsula 63
trout, brown 185
Tryfan, Mount 164
Tudor period 136, 182, 188, 197, 206

Tulloch 112
Turner, J.M.W. 38
Tweed, River 47, **96**
Tweed Valley 47
Tyne, River **92**
Tyne Bridge **92**, 93
Tyneside 93
Tywyn 100

Ullapool 170, 173, **173**
Ulpha 155
UNESCO World Heritage Sites 102, 129, 209, **209**, 224
Union of South Africa steam locomotive 91
Urquhart Castle 231, **231**

Victoria, Queen 95, 131
Victorian period 14, 17, 73, 81, 86, 112, 135, 142, 147, **161**, 196, 203, 209, 216, 217
Vikings 64, 109, 117

Wade, Charles Paget **26**, 28
Wainwright, Alfred 41, **41**
Wales 6, 120, 136, 219
    Cambrian Coast Line **69**, 98–102, **98**, **100**
    Llanberis Pass, Eryri (Snowdonia) National Park **121**, 162–7
    Pembrokeshire Coastal Drive **121**, 156–61
    Snowdon Mountain Railway, Gwynedd 56, **69**, 104–7, **104**, **107**
    South 26
    Yr Wyddfa (Snowdon) Horseshoe 10, **11**, 52–6, **55**, 162
    see also Welsh–English border
walks 6, 7, 9–64
Walton-on-Thames 197
Wansfell Pike 217
Wars of the Roses 140
water voles 36, 39, 209, 225

waterfalls 34, **34**, **36**
Watergate Bay 126
Watling Street 138
Waverton 206
weather, dangers of 54, 55
Webb, Sir Aston 187
well dressing 147
Welsh–English border 219, **219**
    Malvern Hills 138–42
Went Hill Brow 18
West Bay **131**
West Highland Line 7, **69**
    Glasgow to Mallaig 109–12, **109**, **111**, **113**
West Highland Way, The Devil's Staircase **11**, 59–61, **59**, **61**
Westminster Pier 195, **195**
Westmorland 153
Westward Ho! 122, **122**
Wetherlam **41**
Weymouth 131, 133
Whernside 88
White Peak 144, **148**
White Tower 196
Whitebrook 222
Whitesands Bay 157
Widcombe **190**
Widemouth Bay 125
Wigan Pier 213, **213**
Wigmore 138–40
wild flowers 14–17, **14**, 28, 48–50, 133, 225
wild garlic 36, 50, 192–3
William the Conqueror 148, 188, 196
Williamson, Henry 70
willow 73, 78, 204
willowherb 78
Winchcombe 136
Windermere, Lake 40, 42, **42**, 45, **183**, 214–17, **215**, **216**
Windermere Jetty Museum 214
Windrush, River **134**, 135, 136
Windsor 195
Windsor Castle, Round Tower 197, **197**

Winnats Pass **121**, 144, **148**
wood anemones 50
wool trade 135, 208
Wooler 48
Worcester **11**, 24–8, **24**, **69**, 78–81, 138, 142, **142**
Worcester Cathedral 81, **81**, 142
Worcestershire 24, 81, 142
    Malvern Hills **11**, 30–3, **31**, **33**
Worcestershire Beacon 31, **33**
Wordsworth, William 155, **155**, 214, 216, 222
World Water Speed Record 150
Wray Castle 216–17, **216**
Wren, Sir Christopher 133
Wroxham 199–203
Wroxham Bridge **199**
Wrynose Pass **121**, 150–3, **151**, **153**, 155
Wyatt, James 26
Wyche Cutting 31
Wye, River 144, 147, **147**, **183**, 219–22, **219**, **222**

Y Lliwedd ridge 54, 56, **56**
Ye Old Ferrie Inn **221**
Yeo, River 70, 72
Yorkshire 82–5, **83**, **87**, 208–9, **210**
    Craven district 83
    Yorkshire Dales 68, **83**, 209
    Malham Cove **11**, 34–9, **36**
    Settle to Carlisle Railway 68, **69**, 86–91
    Yorkshire Three Peaks 88
Yr Wyddfa (Snowdon) 102, 162
    Snowdon Mountain Railway 56, **69**, 104–7, **104**, **107**
    Horseshoe 10, **11**, 52–6, **55**, 162

All photos are ©Shutterstock, except for the following: 11 Kynance Cove, 35, 216 left (©National Trust Images/Hugh Mothersole); 11 Lindisfarne Castle, 51, 202 bottom (©National Trust Images/Rob Coleman); 11 Cuckmere Haven, 18 (©National Trust Images/Laurence Perry); 12, 46 (©National Trust Images/John Millar); 13, 14 (©National Trust Images/John Miller); 15 (©National Trust Images/Ross Hoddinott); 16 top (©National Trust Images/David Sellman); 16 bottom (©National Trust Images/Sue Brackenbury); 24, 69 Attadale, 69 Barnstaple, 71, 72, 73, 79, 115 bottom, 116, 131, 139 top, 140 left, 142 left, 207 (©Alamy); 27, 28, 189 (©National Trust Images/James Dobson); 38 (©National Trust Images/Paul Harris).